CHRIS BUSH

Chris Bush is an award-winning playwright, lyricist and theatre-maker. Past work includes *Standing at the Sky's Edge* (Sheffield Theatres/National Theatre/West End), *The Odyssey*, *Pericles* (National Theatre: Olivier), *Robin Hood and the Christmas Heist* (Rose Theatre), *Jane Eyre* (Stephen Joseph Theatre/New Vic Theatre), *Fantastically Great Women Who Changed the World* (Kenny Wax, UK tour), *Hungry* (Paines Plough), ~~Kein~~ *Weltuntergang* / ~~Not~~ *The End of the World* (Schaubühne, Berlin), *Nine Lessons and Carols: Stories for a Long Winter* (Almeida Theatre), *Faustus: That Damned Woman* (Headlong/Lyric Hammersmith/Birmingham Rep), *The Last Noël* (Attic Theatre/UK tour), *The Assassination of Katie Hopkins* (Theatr Clwyd), *The Changing Room* (NT Connections), an adaptation of Ibsen's *A Doll's House*, *Rock / Paper / Scissors*, *The Band Plays On*, *Steel*, *What We Wished For*, *A Dream*, *The Sheffield Mysteries* (Sheffield Theatres), *Scenes from the End of the World* (Yard/ Central School), *A Declaration from the People* (National Theatre: Dorfman) and *Larksong* (New Vic, Stoke-on-Trent). Awards include the Hermitage Major Theater Award, an Olivier Award for Best New Musical, a South Bank Sky Arts Award, three UK Theatre Awards, the Perfect Pitch Award, a Brit Writers' Award and the Theatre Royal Haymarket Writers' Award.

Other Titles in this Series

Chris Bush

OTHERLAND

NICK HERN BOOKS
London
www.nickhernbooks.co.uk

A Nick Hern Book

Otherland first published in Great Britain as a paperback original in 2025 by Nick Hern Books Limited, The Glasshouse, 49a Goldhawk Road, London W12 8QP

Otherland copyright © 2025 Chris Bush

Chris Bush has asserted her right to be identified as the author of this work

Front cover: photograph of Jade Anouka and Fizz Sinclair by Phil Fisk; art direction by Studio Doug

Designed and typeset by Nick Hern Books, London
Printed in Great Britain by Mimeo Ltd, Huntingdon, Cambridgeshire PE29 6XX

A CIP catalogue record for this book is available from the British Library

ISBN 978 1 83904 433 5

www.nickhernbooks.co.uk/environmental-policy

Nick Hern Books' authorised representative in the EU is
Easy Access System Europe – Mustamäe tee 50, 10621 Tallinn, Estonia
email gpsr.requests@easproject.com

Otherland was first performed at the Almeida Theatre, London, on 12 February 2025, with the following cast:

JO	Jade Anouka
ELAINE/HERA	Jackie Clune
CHORUS	Danielle Fiamanya
CHORUS	Laura Hanna
CHORUS	Beth Hinton-Lever
CHORUS	Serena Manteghi
HARRY	Fizz Sinclair
GABBY	Amanda Wilkin

BAND
Musical Director/Keyboard	Jennifer Whyte
Harp	Catrin Meek
Cello	Gabriella Swallow

Director	Ann Yee
Set Designer	Fly Davis
Costume Designer	Milla Clarke
Lighting Designer	Anna Watson
Sound Designer	Pete Malkin
Composer and Arranger	Jennifer Whyte
Casting Director	Amy Ball CDG
Costume Supervisor	Heidi Bryan
Voice Coach	Danièle Lydon
Associate Director	Grace Duggan
Dramatherapist	Wabriya King
Company Stage Manager	Julia Reid
Deputy Stage Manager	Sophie Rubenstein
Assistant Stage Manager	Ava McCarthy

Foreword

Otherland is a play almost a decade in the making, although in some ways I've spent a lifetime building up to it. As Harry says: '*I have been searching for you, friends, long before I had any conception of where to look.*' I'm at an extremely privileged point in my career right now where more often than not people approach me with projects – a potential adaptation, a specific brief, an exciting collaboration – but in this instance, it all started with me. That's not to mistake anything here as autobiography – this is categorically a work of fiction – but it's still the most personal thing I've ever written. During the rehearsal process we've talked a lot about theatrical honesty, and an honest play requires an honest introduction.

When I first came out as trans, there was a (mostly well-meaning) presumption that this would have an immediate impact on my work – having embarked on such a zeitgeisty and dramatically rich personal transformation, why would I even bother writing about anything else? I instinctively resisted this – I was still the same person, the same *writer*, interested in the same things, and more to the point, painfully aware that artists can so easily get pigeonholed on the basis of their identities. This wasn't the only reason for my reluctance – more than anything else, I was scared. Time and time again I'd seen how any trans person – particularly any trans woman – with even the smallest amount of public recognition was immediately monstered, ridiculed or harassed the moment they opened their mouths. Living as a trans woman was frightening enough – bringing that into my work just felt like asking for trouble.

Being honest though, I *had* changed – to pretend I hadn't would be absurd. My experience of the world and my own precarious position within it was shifting, I was actively unlearning decades of assumptions and privileges, and yes, perhaps for the first time my lived experience contained something worth writing about. Furthermore, *not* writing or openly talking about this aspect of my identity was becoming its own frustration, not entirely dissimilar to the frustration I'd felt for all those years before I came out. Despite all this, I was still very wary of writing my Big Trans Play™ , even if there were a number of theatres interested in commissioning it. I set myself some loose ground rules: it had to be about more than just trans identity, it had to be theatrically expansive and full of ideas, it couldn't be simple, it couldn't be easily dismissed as navel-gazing life writing, it had to be as good as I had the capacity to make it. I challenged myself to be honest, to press on my bruises where I had to, to write with a vulnerability I probably never had before. Of course it had to have joy and gags and life in it too – it needed to be a roller-coaster, not a slog.

I like to describe theatre as a machine for empathy – there is, in my opinion, no better medium for making people care about things. We gather in the dark to watch people who are like us but also not like us play out a story, we see a window into a different world, we imagine a different point of view. For this reason, I also knew this couldn't be an angry or a hectoring play, full of resentments and accusations. Instead, I hope it can be taken as a plea for understanding. It is a play about womanhood in all its myriad forms, and all the unspoken rules, unfair restrictions and unreasonable demands that come with it. Through Jo and Harry, we meet two women who are trying to rediscover themselves after a lifetime spent following other people's instructions. Neither of them are perfect, but they're doing their best. Their stories are worth telling.

Of course, a play a decade in the making doesn't get anywhere without countless kind souls shepherding it on its way. I'm hugely grateful to Ann Yee for bringing it so gloriously to life, along with Jen, Fly, Milla, Anna, Pete, Amy, Heidi, Danièle and Grace, our unbeatable stage management, technical and production teams; our extraordinary cast: Fizz, Jade, Amanda, Jackie, Beth, Danielle, Serena and Laura (and superstar stand-in Eleanor Sutton); everyone at the Almeida, from Rupert and Steph down; every actor who took part in a workshop along the way; Guy Jones, who I first developed the idea with, and Clare Slater, who picked up that torch; the wonderful team at Nick Hern Books; and my ever-patient agents Matt and Alex at Berlin. I also need to thank Roni, my wonderful partner, and my always supportive family. It's very important to get into print that my own mother is *nothing* like Elaine.

When I was last at the Almeida, it was the winter of 2020 and we were (very cautiously) just starting to pick ourselves up again after a year of chaos. Yes, admittedly, the production in question (*Nine Lessons and Carols: Stories for a Long Winter*) was closed the day after we opened as London entered another tier of lockdown, but it remains one of my happiest theatre-making experiences. The joy and gratitude we all felt simply to be back in a room making work will always stick with me. There is no place I'd rather open *Otherland* than here, and I'm endlessly thankful that they were bold enough to programme it. This is a play I needed to write – I can only hope it finds the people who need to see it.

Chris Bush
February 2025

Characters

CHORUS 1	DOCTOR 2
CHORUS 2	MAN
CHORUS 3	DOCTOR 3
CHORUS 4	TECHNICIAN
JO	CAPTAIN
HARRY	BOSUN
EVE	PROFESSOR
LILY	HERA
RUTH	WAITRESS
LEIGH	
ELAINE	
TESSA	
RECEPTIONIST	
DOCTOR 1	
TATTOOIST	
WOMAN	
JEN	
MOIRA	
CLERK	
DOCUMENTARIAN	
ASSISTANT	
TEENAGER	
GABBY	
GAYLE	
ASH	
MAYA	
BETH	

Written for an all-female cast. **HARRY** *must be played by
a trans woman. She is only ever represented as a woman.
The broader casting should always aim to present as diverse
a picture of womanhood as possible.*

Suggested Doubling for Eight Actors

1. JO

2. HARRY

3. GABBY

4. ELAINE, HERA, WAITRESS

5. CHORUS 1, EVE, RECEPTIONIST, JEN, ASH, CAPTAIN

6. CHORUS 2, LILY, WOMAN, CLERK, TEENAGER, BOSUN

7. CHORUS 3, RUTH, TESSA, TATTOOIST, GAYLE, MAN, DOCTOR 3, PROFESSOR, DOCUMENTARIAN

8. CHORUS 4, LEIGH, DOCTOR 1 *and* 2, MOIRA, ASSISTANT, MAYA, BETH, TECHNICIAN

This text went to press before the end of rehearsals and so may differ slightly from the play as performed.

ACT ONE

1.

HARRY and JO *are getting married. They are extraordinarily happy. Music plays as* JO *walks down the aisle, something akin to Pachelbel's Canon. All their friends are there. They speak to us as* CHORUS.

CHORUS 2. This is Jo

CHORUS 1. And this is Harry

CHORUS 3. And they are in love.

CHORUS 4. They are beautiful.

CHORUS 3. They are unbearable.

CHORUS 1. They are the best of us. Hashtag-couples-goals.

CHORUS 2. Their love is a blinding, brilliant, beautiful thing.

CHORUS 4. And it is a privilege to witness.

The music moves rapidly through various different forms: a romantic first dance, a wild ceilidh, a late-night disco. Full of energy and excitement and love. HARRY *and* JO *could take on the world right now. Then another shift – something stranger, ominous, foreboding:*

CHORUS.
YOU ARE MY ANCHOR
WEIGH ME DOWN
YOU ARE MY ANCHOR
WEIGH ME DOWN

DON'T LET ME DRIFT AWAY
DRIFT AWAY, DRIFT AWAY
HOLD ME TIGHT
HOLD ME TOO TIGHTLY

Then as abruptly as it started, the moment ends. We return to the uplift and ecstasy of the wedding disco, as the GUESTS *head off into the night. Sharply into –*

2.

Years later. JO *and* HARRY *are amidst boxes.* JO *holds a piece of crockery.*

JO. I think that's everything from the kitchen.

HARRY. Right.

JO. We have so much shit. When did that happen?

HARRY. It just happens, doesn't it? You accumulate shit.

JO. *You* accumulate. You hoard. (*Holding up the crockery.*) This is the ugliest thing I've ever seen in my life.

HARRY. Be nice. My sister gave us that.

JO. Really? (*Trying hard to make* HARRY *laugh.*) What a stone-cold bitch.

HARRY *smiles.*

What happened to the big red one? Wasn't there like a big red one – big, rectangular, for… like for lasagne and things?

HARRY. I've not seen anything like that.

JO. Yeah, but have you just done man-looking? (*Beat.*) Sorry.

HARRY. That's –

JO. I'm sorry.

HARRY. It's okay. Um. I'll, uh, if anything like that turns up –

JO (*putting the crockery down*). Don't worry about it.

HARRY. Any stuff you want –

JO. I don't. (*Beat.*) I really don't. Stuff is… oppressive. I don't even think I want internet in my new place.

HARRY. What?

JO. I mean it – I just want my CDs, that's all. (*Beat.*) Have you gone through yours yet? We could do it now? We don't have to, but I would like to get it done, and I don't want to take stuff that's yours – anything you think is yours –

HARRY. Yeah.

JO. And I know you say you don't mind, you say 'take anything' now, but –

HARRY. Yeah, we can look at CDs. Sure.

JO. I'm not enjoying this either.

HARRY. I know.

JO. I'm not trying to upset you.

HARRY. I know.

JO. I love you. (*Beat.*) Harry? I do. I still –

HARRY. Then what are we doing here? Because if that's true –

JO. Don't –

HARRY. No one's making us do this.

JO. We can finish up another time. You can go through CDs by yourself, when you're less upset.

HARRY. Just –

JO. But you do have to do it. You have to accept that this is happening. You have to respect me when I –

HARRY. What if we just pressed pause? What if we… we… took the pressure off, put everything in storage, bought some breathing space to –

JO. Harry –

HARRY. To… to re-evaluate, re-acclimatise –

JO. That isn't –

HARRY. We could go away somewhere.

JO. What?

HARRY. I could stop. (*Pause.*) What if I stopped? Not, not forever, but –

JO. Don't do this.

HARRY. If I pressed pause?

JO. Stop it.

HARRY. Ask me to stop and I'll stop.

JO. It isn't fair to me when you do this.

HARRY. Because we... we... we have to try, don't we? Jo? You owe me that.

JO. I should go. This was a bad idea. I was hoping we could be adults and friends and not one of those couples – those *ex*-couples who... But you know what, forget it, just keep them all. It's only stuff.

She starts to go.

HARRY. Wait.

JO *stops.*

Wait, just –

JO *turns back round.*

JO. Fuck it. No, I won't just... These are mine. (*She picks up CDs at random.*) Annie Lennox – mine, David Bowie – mine, TLC – mine. These are the only things I've asked for. And you won't even play them! They'll just sit here gathering dust, and... you don't get everything. You don't get to keep everything as some compensation for... Don't. Don't just... This is what you do – you stand there like some wounded animal and you put everything on me, so I'm the one who has to... I'm the monster, I'm the bad guy, and you just *stand there*, and what it means is you end up with everything you wanted. Fuck it. Say something.

HARRY (*softly*). Do you think this is everything I wanted?

JO. I'm sorry, I am, but I can't keep going over… I can't do this. I can't. (*She softens.*) I, uh, I've left a bag on the dresser too. Some jewellery and make-up and other bits and pieces, stuff I never use. You can chuck it, donate it, do whatever, but it's going to be expensive, starting everything over.

HARRY. Yeah.

JO. I'm sorry.

HARRY. You have to have the internet.

JO. Why?

HARRY. Because you have to! How else are you going to do anything?

JO. I don't know – with my hands, maybe? With my fucking hands. To feel something again. (*Beat.*) Do you know where you're moving to yet? (*Beat.*) You should start looking. I want you to find somewhere nice.

Straight into –

3.

JO *and* HARRY *remain onstage. The* CHORUS *come forward to tell their story.*

CHORUS 2. This is Jo

CHORUS 1. And this is Harry

CHORUS 3. And they were in love once. We know – we were there.

CHORUS 4. They were happy and they were beautiful.

CHORUS 3. Met at university, married five years later, never one of the couples we had to worry about.

CHORUS 1. But a lot has happened since then. A lot of ground to cover between swearing vows and divvying up the Le Creuset.

CHORUS 4. We're still trying to make sense of it.

CHORUS 2. So lately they've both been getting a lot of –

The CHORUS *now become various friends* (EVE, RUTH *and* LEIGH) *addressing* JO *and* HARRY.

EVE. Fuck.

RUTH. Okay.

LEIGH. Wow. Really?

RUTH. Right. Great.

EVE. Fuck. I'm sorry, but fuck.

CHORUS 2. Because Jo and Harry are changing.
And we respect that.
Change is important too.

LEIGH. I don't get it. Honestly, I just don't get it.

RUTH. Sorry. I don't know what to say.

EVE. I don't know what I'm allowed to ask but –

HARRY. Oh. Anything, within reason.

A flood of questions – some to HARRY, *some to* JO.

EVE. So how do you know?

LEIGH. When did you know?

RUTH. When did you tell her?

EVE. What did you tell her?

RUTH. Does e*veryone* know?

LEIGH. What did he say?

EVE. And what happens now?

CHORUS 2. Which is maybe the wrong question –
    A vast, unanswerable question.
    Jo and Harry are changing.
    Harry is changing more than most, undeniably,
    And change is beautiful. Necessary. Terrifying.
    No way of knowing where it'll leave them.

JO. It isn't just about that.

RUTH. No. Of course.

HARRY. She says it isn't about that.

EVE. Uh-huh.

JO. But it's still a lot to –

LEIGH. Yeah. Obviously, yeah.

CHORUS 3. Jo and Harry are changing.
    And if we're being honest – one hundred per cent honest
    We're a little bit annoyed that we're only finding out about
    this now.
    Because Harry's been carrying her secret for a lifetime
    Told Jo over a decade ago,
    The first time she'd told anyone
    Finally shared her deepest, darkest sordid shame –

HARRY. It isn't really –

CHORUS 2. Because Jo was special, that's the point.
    Jo *is* special, the kind of person you'd risk everything for,
    And so a full ten years before we got wind of it –

CHORUS 4. Despite the fact they'd only really just met –

CHORUS 1. They'd barely started dating –

CHORUS 3. Harry was about to head off to the other side of the
    world –

CHORUS 2. Despite all this, or maybe because of it,
    Harry took the leap, and –

    We jump back in time.

JO (*to* HARRY). What does that mean?

HARRY. I...

JO. You want to be...?

HARRY. I think... I don't know if 'want' is... Want, or that
I should've been – that I would've been happier if I was...

JO (*finishing it for her*). A woman? (*Pause.*) You think you're
a woman?

HARRY. Is that...? I'm not... I know it isn't... I know I can't...

JO. As like a sex thing? A dress-up thing?

HARRY. No!

JO. Right. Sorry.

HARRY. It's not –

JO. I'm sorry. (*Beat.*) How long have you...?

HARRY. Oh, um... years. Years and years. Ever since... It's
been a long time.

JO. Okay.

HARRY. I'm sorry.

JO. That's okay.

HARRY (*as quickly as she can*). And I think – what I think is –
I don't think I'll ever do anything about it. I don't think
I could... Um. This isn't the whole reason, but practically,
realistically, I look at myself and I don't see how I could ever
get to a point that'd be... acceptable, I suppose. Not
ridiculous, worth all the... Which might seem shallow, but it is
a legitimate... I wouldn't want to be a... a freak. Paint a target
on my... And I can live with it – live like this – I think I've
made peace with it, to an extent, so I could've just never told
you, like I've never told anyone, and it's not the end of the
world, but it is a thing about me, a thing that I don't think is
ever going away, and... I wanted you to know. I'm not asking
you for anything, but I think this thing between us means more

than either of us have been admitting, so I thought it was only fair that you should know.

JO. But you don't want to do anything?

HARRY. No. Not now, anyway.

JO. Okay. (*Beat.*) Talk to me, if that changes.

HARRY. Yeah?

JO. Yeah. (*Beat. She tries to play it down.*) You know I like girls too – I normally go for… It's not a big deal, I promise.

HARRY. Okay.

JO. And 'this thing between us'?

HARRY. You don't have to –

JO. We should find out what it is. If you want to. And we'll keep checking in on the other thing – if you want to. (*Beat.*) Come here.

JO *kisses* HARRY. *The moment ends.*

CHORUS 4. We have heard a version of this story so many times. The edited version.

CHORUS 2. 'This thing between us means more than either of us have been admitting'

CHORUS 1. The poetry of it. The courage.

CHORUS 4. But never the full story.

CHORUS 1. You see Harry was never meant to stay –
Harry had a masters programme lined up in Rhode Island – fully funded.
Harry had a whole life waiting for her, across the ocean
Her mother, newly divorced, already relocated
Starting fresh adventures of her own
But Jo put an end to all that –

CHORUS 3. *Love* put an end to it.
This thing between them means more than either of them have been admitting, so what else can they do?

They commit, cohabit, marry.
Hashtag-couples-goals, and happily ever after.

CHORUS 4. And as for the *other thing* –
Jo does keep checking in, just like she promised.
It's Harry who never wants to talk about it.
Finds it awkward, excruciating, impossible –
What's there to say, when there's nothing to be done?
And she swears she wasn't *always* unhappy,
Not every minute of every hour of every day,
But it is always there; an ever-present drip, a spreading stain,
Gradually building a new ocean within her.
An ocean between them.
And now, a decade later –

Back in dialogue. The present. HARRY *and* EVE.

EVE. So why now?

HARRY. Oh.

EVE. Sorry – you don't have to.

HARRY. No, it's… It wasn't one thing. I just kept waiting for it
to get easier, and it never did, and somewhere the scales
tipped. The idea of never doing anything felt worse than
doing something, y'know?

EVE. Yeah. Well no, but –

HARRY. And Jo's always said whenever I was ready, y'know?
I think I can really picture it now – picture it with her –

EVE. Yeah. I mean thank fuck for Jo.

HARRY. Yeah. Thank fuck.

The moment ends.

CHORUS 3. And there is a moment, this incredible fleeting
moment of yeah, fuck it, maybe they'll be fine – maybe
they'll be better than ever – Harry genuinely believes this.

CHORUS 4. But then there's Jo, who has to find this –

JO. Brilliant, but –

CHORUS 4. Forced to find this –

JO. Incredible, but –

CHORUS 4. No choice but to find all this –

JO. Beautiful. Really actually beautiful, but –

CHORUS 4. Jo is being squeezed out of her own story
    Relegated to a supporting role
    Now everyone's attention is on –

HARRY is back with RUTH *and* LILY, *two other friends.*

RUTH. And you're sticking with 'Harry'?

HARRY. Yeah. Uh, Harriet, officially – legally – on any
    paperwork.

LILY. Do you think you're cool enough to be a girl Harry? I feel
    like girl Harrys are cool.

HARRY. Right. Fair.

Now EVE *joins the conversation.*

EVE. No, because to be honest, I don't think I ever really
    thought of you as a man. Not like a *man*-man.

RUTH. Yes, exactly!

EVE. In a good way – like a really good way.

LILY (*to* HARRY). And is Jo coming out later? How's she
    doing?

The conversations now overlap. JO *is with* LEIGH; HARRY
    with EVE, RUTH *and* LILY.

JO. I'm okay.

HARRY (*to* LILY). She's good. Great.

LEIGH (*to* JO). You're sure?

HARRY. You know Jo likes girls – likes women – almost
    always dated –

LILY. Right.

HARRY. So it's not a problem.

Focus falls solely on JO *and* LEIGH.

LEIGH (*still to* JO). But he told you he'd never do anything?

JO. *She.*

LEIGH. Yeah, but you never agreed to – ?

JO. I don't think I have to agree. If he – if *she* – if Harry... God, and if you've seen her... She's terrified, of course she is, but it's like this weight... I can't tell her not to. I don't *want* her not to, I just... Harry should do whatever Harry needs to do, right? Whatever that means for us.

Suddenly HARRY *is in front of* JO. *Her heart has just been broken. She is shellshocked.*

HARRY. You said this was okay – it was allowed –

JO. I said you should do it – of course you should do it, if that's what you need to... This isn't about that.

HARRY. Then what?

JO. I'm tired – can we talk about this in the morning?

HARRY. No – you keep saying it's not about this, not about me... So what is it then? If it's not about *this*, then what?

CHORUS 2. And Jo doesn't know what to tell her,
Because it isn't just one thing,
But all this time an ocean has been building within her too,
An ocean she is only just beginning to comprehend the scale of.

JO. Fuck.

CHORUS 2. Jo sees the breadth of eternity stretching out before her,
Eternity with a woman she's now wondering if she ever really knew –
And a vanishingly small window through which to escape.

JO. Can't it be about me? What *I* need, what I… We haven't been working, have we? How could we, with you lying about… Not *lying*, but denying something as big as… I'm not angry with you. Maybe I am. But I haven't been happy either, not for… That's what it's about. I should get to be happy too.

CHORUS 2. This is Jo

CHORUS 1. And this is Harry

CHORUS 3. And they were beautiful. The best of us.

CHORUS 4. And who knows what they are now?

CHORUS.
SALTWATER SPILLS OUT OF ME
YOU PLUG MY LEAKS
MAKE ME WHOLE
WHEN YOU HOLD ONTO ME
MAKE ME COMPLETE

YOU ARE MY ANCHOR
WEIGH ME DOWN

Straight into –

4.

HARRY *is having a phone conversation with* ELAINE, *her mother.*

HARRY. I'll figure it out. There's still a month left on the lease.

ELAINE. And you can't just stay where you are? Just until Jo – ?

HARRY. Not by myself.

ELAINE. If it's about money –

HARRY. No, it's… I don't know if I'd want to stay here by myself.

ELAINE. Well maybe it's time for you to finally come visit us. Maybe you could take some leave, jump on a plane, and –

HARRY (*non-committal*). Yeah.

ELAINE. Try not to sound too wildly enthusiastic about seeing your dear old mother.

HARRY. No, I would, it's just I think I need to be near Jo, just for whatever... And there's work too, we're in the middle of a grant proposal.

ELAINE. Yes, you said you were speaking to what's-her-name – your head of department?

HARRY. Oh, Tessa, yeah. It'll be fine. It's just a lot of paperwork, really.

ELAINE. So you're definitely...? At work you'll be working as – ?

HARRY. I don't want to drag it out. I think I just need to be out to everyone, everywhere or it's going to drive me crazy.

ELAINE. And that's all allowed, is it?

HARRY. They can't stop me.

ELAINE. I still want you to come see us – in the summer, maybe. It's absurd you've still never met Michael in person. I know you don't like flying. Get a ferry if you have to. Take a cruise. Swim.

HARRY. I'll try. I'll need a passport first, but –

ELAINE. What do you mean?

HARRY. Doesn't matter. Leave it with me.

ELAINE. Why don't you have a passport? You can renew them online. It's not –

HARRY. No, it's... I still have my old one, but I'll need... I'll need a new passport as... A passport I can travel under *now*, so...

ELAINE. Oh.

HARRY. Yeah.

ELAINE. But that's not – ?

HARRY. I did look into it, actually. You need a letter – a doctor's letter – but it has to be from a specialist, not a GP, and you can't just make an appointment, you have to get referred, and I think that has happened now, but it'll still be actual years before I see anyone, so –

ELAINE. Years?

HARRY. Yeah. Well decades, actually, going by… People are getting their first appointments now who were referred five, six years ago –

ELAINE. Five years?

HARRY. Yeah. Depending on –

ELAINE. That can't be right.

HARRY. But more people are getting referred now, and they can't keep up with it, so the lists just keep growing and growing, and they keep saying they're going to reform things, or they used to say that, anyway, but the government hates us – well, everyone hates us, actually – so who knows what's going on, it's all just getting worse, and the private places are all booked up too.

ELAINE. Right.

HARRY. Sorry, do you mind me talking about…?

ELAINE. But you can still use…? Your old passport – it's not expired?

HARRY. Sorry?

ELAINE. It's still valid, isn't it? It's still you. Legally. (*Pause.*) Are you there?

HARRY. Yes. Yeah, I'm here.

ELAINE. So you're going to have to… For work, as well – don't they want to send you to Barbados?

HARRY. Bermuda. Maybe. If we get the funding.

ELAINE. Right. You can't miss that.

HARRY. It's still work – it's not a holiday.

ELAINE. I just mean you can't put your entire life on hold
for... I think you're going to have to be realistic. You might
have to compromise.

HARRY. Let me think about it. Um. Let me see what I can do.

ELAINE. Okay. (*Beat*.) And can I ask about Jo?

On a separate part of the stage, a RECEPTIONIST *appears.*

RECEPTIONIST. Mrs Albany?

JO enters.

ELAINE. Because it can't be easy for her.

HARRY. Yeah.

RECEPTIONIST (*to* JO). Just take a seat. Won't be long.

The RECEPTIONIST *goes.* JO *waits.*

ELAINE. So... So... I'm just going to say this: If you stopped –
if you didn't do this, or... or you just slowed down – because
it's all been very sudden.

HARRY. It hasn't. Jo's known since –

ELAINE. Yes, but if in practice... If it's something she can't
live with –

HARRY. It's about what I can live with.

ELAINE. But it would make things easier, wouldn't it? It'd
have to.

HARRY. Yeah.

ELAINE. So you do *need* to do this? (*Beat*.) Harry? It's really
necessary?

A snap into –

5.

JO *is now with a* DOCTOR, *mid-consultation*. HARRY *and* ELAINE *go*.

JO. It's necessary to me.

DOCTOR 1. Are you experiencing any bleeding, bloating, dizziness, nausea?

JO. No, but –

DOCTOR 1. Complications from the contraceptive implant are rare – especially when you've been using it for as long as you have.

JO. It's not about that.

DOCTOR 1. But you're not trying to get pregnant?

JO. No, I'm not. Absolutely not. No.

DOCTOR 1. Are you sexually active?

JO. Not right at this second. (*Beat*.) Um. I'm in the process of separating from my... my husband, I suppose. That's weird to say. I'm not –

DOCTOR 1. I'm sorry to hear that.

JO. Thank you.

DOCTOR 1. Have you given any thought to egg storage?

JO (*thrown*). I'm sorry?

DOCTOR 1. It's worth considering, if you're not looking to start a family just yet. Women in your position often think they have all the time in the world, but in reality –

JO. I have no intention of getting pregnant. I never want to get pregnant. Ever.

DOCTOR 1. Understood. In which case the implant remains extremely effective.

JO (*bluntly*). I like women. (*Beat*.) Um. I'm actually fairly certain I'm almost entirely a lesbian, so if I'm sleeping with anyone, I think it'll be with women – going forward. Or a woman, singular. One step at a time.

DOCTOR 1. I see. Well, as there is only a year – a little over a year until your implant is due to be replaced, I suggest we revisit it then –

JO. But I don't want it.

DOCTOR 1. Of course if you do find yourself in the position of wanting to conceive –

JO. I don't like having it in me.

DOCTOR 1. But it hasn't been causing you any problems?

JO. I don't know! I don't know if… I've had it since I was fifteen – *fifteen* – that's my entire adult life, leeching out this… changing my… I don't even know who I was before you put this in me – that's the problem! I've read about it – how it effects behaviour, emotion, attraction – it's the Borg, it's the Cybermen – I let them put this little bit of robot inside me because I couldn't be trusted to just think for myself, basically, and I've had enough of it.

DOCTOR 1. And I see here you're on a waiting list for NHS counselling.

JO. I'm not mad. I just don't like having something in me that could be making me something I'm not. I want to be in control. I want to know who I am. I just want it out, please. Can you just take it out of me?

Scene ends. Into –

6.

JO *leaves the doctor's office, taking out an old-school CD Walkman and headphones from her bag.*

CHORUS 3. And soon Jo has an almost invisible scar on her upper arm
Where that robot part of her has been removed
Where a little piece of herself was reclaimed
A tiny battle won

JO *presses play – music starts.*

And opts to mark the occasion
Through the inking of three small blobs in its place
Which signify –

Cut straight into JO *in a tattoo parlour with a* TATTOOIST, *midway through.* JO *is wincing throughout, and the pain might occasionally break her line of thought.*

JO. Because I'm free now, yeah? I'm unplugged.

TATTOOIST. Mmm.

JO. Have you ever done a plug socket before?

TATTOOIST. No.

JO. Do you think it's stupid?

TATTOOIST. No.

JO. My mum's gonna hate it.

TATTOOIST. Yeah?

JO. Oh yeah, for sure. But you know what they say – a bad decision is better than no decision at all.

TATTOOIST. Do people say that?

JO. They should. And this, it's about… liberation, right? About how we're all plugged into this… wired up to all this… this fucking hivemind, this all-knowing algorithm telling us what to do, how to feel, who to fuck – *fuck*!

TATTOOIST. Just try and keep your arm really still for me.

JO. Sorry.

TATTOOIST. Pain okay?

JO. Yeah. Do your worst. Fuck me up. And Harry – that's my ex, Harry – she made a decision – fair play to her. She couldn't live how she was living so she said fuck it, she unplugged, and… you know what? She did me the biggest favour, because she made me realise we'd both been pretending, and… and she is so scared.

TATTOOIST. Yeah?

JO. Yeah. Of course yeah. And here I am, worst person in the world, because I've abandoned her – just left her to deal with all of… You know she's only here because of me – that's the story we tell everyone – she only stayed in the country for me, had this whole other life planned, but then we fell in love, and… and it's bullshit too, actually. She stayed because she's terrified of flying and her mum is a lot and… I was convenient, that's all. But not this time. I can't just be along for somebody else's ride. I'm in control now.

TATTOOIST. You're done.

JO. I am so fucking done.

TATTOOIST. No, I mean you're finished – I'm finished with your –

JO. Oh, right. Great. That was quick.

CHORUS.
    PULL ME APART
    SEVER ALL TIES
    BRING ON THE PAIN
    I AM WAITING FOR –

    COLOUR ME IN
    I AM ALIVE
    EACH INCH OF MY SKIN
    HAS BEEN WAITING FOR –

JO *leaves the tattoo parlour and is now out drinking with* LEIGH.

JO. One more.

LEIGH. I can't.

JO. You can.

LEIGH. Tom's going to be waiting.

JO. So what? Fuck Tom. Let him wait.

LEIGH. Come on –

JO. You know Harry's waiting – waiting for me to come to my senses, and… (*Suddenly a bit more serious.*) I'm not going back to her.

LEIGH. I know.

JO. I can't.

LEIGH. I'm getting you an Uber.

JO. I'm not going home. I don't think I'm ever going home.

CHORUS.
ONWARD AND ONWARD
AND ONWARD AND ONWARD
ONWARD AND ONWARD
AND ONWARD AND ONWARD

Music swells. JO *dances. The* CHORUS *forms around her. The beat grows more pronounced.*

CHORUS 4. Jo is making up for lost time.

CHORUS 3. She doesn't need us right now
Doesn't want our sympathy, our pity or our food parcels.

CHORUS 1. Harry was always the cook. But Harry is –

CHORUS 3. Jo is not in mourning.
Jo is not some incapable widower –
Jo is living her best damn life.

JO (*on the dance floor*). I am living my best damn life.

CHORUS 4. And that is cause for celebration, not concern.

CHORUS 1. And if we are concerned –

> JO *is talking to a* WOMAN *in the club, shouting over music. She's definitely been drinking.*

JO. Then fuck them! You know how sometimes you do just have to say fuck your friends? Cos I am, y'know – I am thirty, for fuck's sake – thirty-*something* – and that is too young for pottering. That is my prime! A plague on all your farmers' markets! Fuck you, and your *Guardian Weekend* lives. I was never like them. I'm leaving the city soon. I'm going off-grid.

WOMAN. Yeah?

JO. Yeah. I'm going to quit my job and build a cabin in the forest.

WOMAN. Oh – have you seen the lesbian lumberjack on TikTok?

JO. No! Fuck TikTok! Fuck any of that. *Unplugged.* I'm going to find some corner of the forest – some fucking deep, dark corner where no one has ever been before, and I'm going to plant a flag in the earth. I'm going to find somewhere that's *mine*. What do you think? Just dance with me then.

CHORUS 4. Jo goes all in.
Jo throws shapes like she's trying to shed her skin
And something like the last ten years of domesticity.

CHORUS 2. Jo dances her way out of her body.

CHORUS 1. Jo stays out too late.

CHORUS 3. Jo feels the fear and does it anyway.

CHORUS 2. Jo gets a septum piercing and gets fucked on MDMA with a Glaswegian bull dyke in a composting toilet at a midscale music festival.

CHORUS 1. Jo dodges our calls.

CHORUS 4. Jo is fine.

CHORUS 3. Jo is looking fine.

CHORUS 1. Jo is a fox.

CHORUS 4. Or a shark. If she stops moving, she might drown.

CHORUS.
  PULL ME APART
  SEVER ALL TIES
  ASK ME TO DANCE
  I'VE BEEN WAITING FOR –

  BUY ME A DRINK
  SHOW ME A GOOD TIME
  THE SWEAT ON YOUR SKIN
  HAS ME WAITING FOR

  I AM WAITING FOR, WAITING FOR –

A snap into another scene. JO *with a work colleague,* JEN.

JEN. Peru?

JO. Uh-huh.

JEN. Like Paddington?

JO. The Inca Trail.

JEN. Right. (*Beat.*) So did you want to put in a request for
  remote working, or…

  JO *laughs.*

  You'd be surprised what they can accommodate these days.
  They call it digital nomads – as long as you've got Wi-Fi –

JO. I'm not… I won't be on Wi-Fi – I'll be in *Peru*.

JEN. Yeah, it's just not a great time.

JO. Then I quit. (*Beat.*) I mean it.

JEN. Are you feeling okay?

JO. You know I was going to do something once. I was going to write and paint and build a fucking cabin in the forest. I'm going to go to Peru, and if I don't have a job by the time I get back, I'll deal with that later. I'll send you a postcard.

JO goes. Music stops abruptly. Into –

7.

HARRY is with TESSA, her head of department. Everything much quieter, stiller here.

TESSA. So I think I've got everything I need. Payroll have some questions. Are you okay to pick up with Sally?

HARRY. Sure.

TESSA. And I've put together an email just to warn… (*She corrects herself.*) Just so everyone knows what to expect. (*Beat.*) Now I do still have you down to lead inductions next month, and there's the marine-life panel in Colchester. Richard's said he's happy to step in, if you'd rather.

HARRY. No, that's fine, it's my paper.

TESSA. Yes. I just didn't know whether you'd rather… If you preferred to stay in the lab, avoid some of the more public, the front-facing –

HARRY. No, that's… I'd like to keep everything going as normal, please.

TESSA. Whatever you think's best.

HARRY. Is that okay?

TESSA. If that's your decision. (*Beat.*) Now – just one other thing. I did want a chat about bathrooms, just briefly.

HARRY. Oh?

TESSA. As you know, our facilities are all a bit medieval, but chemistry have finished their big refurb now.

HARRY. Yeah.

TESSA. So everything on their ground floor, that's all unisex, disabled, single use – not single *use* – you know what I mean. So I think that's easiest.

HARRY. You don't want me – ?

TESSA. Much nicer than anything we've got here.

HARRY. Right.

TESSA. Just for everyone's comfort, and to give you some privacy.

HARRY. Right.

TESSA. Smashing. I think you're being very brave.

A shift. Now HARRY *is back with* EVE *and* LILY, *as* TESSA *disappears.*

EVE. No, fuck that. I would've kicked off.

HARRY. She's right – they are nicer.

LILY. Yeah, but –

HARRY. She's been pretty good actually.

EVE. She's telling you where to piss.

HARRY. I don't really use toilets when I'm out anyway.

LILY. What, not ever?

EVE. How does that work?

HARRY. I... I just hold it until –

EVE. Nah, no way – come with us.

HARRY. What's happening?

EVE. We're going to the loo together – it's what girls do. Then we're getting shots. Don't even think of answering back. Captain's orders.

HARRY (*giving in/playing along*). Aye-aye, captain.

EVE *and* LILY *haul* HARRY *up, pulling her straight into* MOIRA, *an academic administrator. Another shift and* EVE *is gone.* MOIRA *is a little confused.*

MOIRA. Oh, right. Hello!

HARRY. That panel is today?

MOIRA. Yes, yes. And you're from Imperial?

HARRY. That's right.

MOIRA. Here we are – something's got jumbled. I was expecting a Harriet – Dr Harriet Albany.

HARRY. Yes, that's –

MOIRA (*cheerfully*). Not you, obviously! So what name am I looking for?

Before HARRY *can respond, she's back with* TESSA *again.* MOIRA *goes.*

TESSA. How was it? It's Norman, isn't it – Colchester? With some Roman bits?

HARRY. I'm not sure.

TESSA. But it was all…?

HARRY. Yeah – fine.

TESSA. Did you get my email about Durham, and the frogs?

HARRY. Yes – did you mean to…? Amphibians are more Eduardo's thing.

TESSA (*with a well-meaning enthusiasm*). No, no, but they're the sex-change frogs! Reed frogs – African –

HARRY. Right.

TESSA. So I thought you'd... Fascinating. They can just spontaneously... Must make you jealous! Anyway, there's a paper at a conference in Durham. I could sign you up?

A CLERK *appears*. TESSA *goes again*.

CLERK. With an 'i'?

HARRY. Harri with an 'i', yes. Like in Harriet.

CLERK. I don't have that name on the system.

HARRY. Yes, that's what I'm trying to change.

CLERK. And do you have some photo ID?

HARRY. No. Well yes, but not in... That's why –

CLERK. Okay, Mr Albany. I'm going to fetch my supervisor.

The CLERK *goes. Into a* RECEPTIONIST.

RECEPTIONIST. We aren't taking new referrals, I'm afraid. I can put you on our waiting list.

A SHOP ASSISTANT.

ASSISTANT. Sir? Sorry, sir, the men's changing rooms are upstairs.

A husky-voiced DOCUMENTARIAN *provides a snippet of voice-over.*

DOCUMENTARIAN....Animals that switch sex as adults are known as sequential hermaphrodites, as opposed to simultaneous hermaphrodites, who –

A TEENAGER *to a friend.*

TEENAGER. Oh my God don't stare.

We hear a recorded message from JO.

JO (*pre-recorded*). Hi, you've reached Jo – I can't come to the phone or I'm screening my calls. Leave a message and I'll get back to you.

Back to TESSA. HARRY *is deflated.*

TESSA. So I'll ask Richard to fill in?

HARRY. Yeah. Just this once. Just until –

TESSA. No pressure. Whatever you think's best.

HARRY. Thank you.

TESSA. It's good work – really good. You should be proud of it.

HARRY. Thank you.

TESSA. Loughborough is a dump. You're not missing anything.

HARRY. Yeah.

TESSA (*kindly*). You come find me, if you need anything else. Anything at all.

Another shift. HARRY *is back with* ELAINE. *Another phone conversation.*

ELAINE. You got the save-the-date?

HARRY. I did – thank you.

ELAINE. I never knew Michael had so much family. His brother's coming all the way from New Zealand. Everyone's making an effort.

HARRY. Yeah.

ELAINE. And it's after Bermuda, so you'll have sorted something by then.

HARRY. I might not be going any more.

ELAINE. What?

HARRY. It's such a long way. It's a budget thing, mostly. We're talking to a lab in Oban instead.

ELAINE. Oban?

HARRY. Scotland. Proper state-of-the-art – and I'd only have to take a train.

ELAINE. Harry –

HARRY. And we've got carbon targets, climate pledges too –

ELAINE. The wedding – I think Mike would really appreciate it if you made an effort. And Rachel's a good kid – she likes you.

HARRY. I like her.

ELAINE. It's important. I've only just got past being the wicked stepmother. So will you work something out, please?

HARRY. Yeah.

ELAINE. And just come as you are – as you are, do you hear me? It's family.

HARRY. I'll try.

Into –

8.

A shift. HARRY *stays,* ELAINE *goes and* CHORUS *appear. Music plays.*

CHORUS 3. And Harry is trying
Everyone is trying, actually
And she buckles under the weight of their accumulated effort.

CHORUS 1. Harry's shoulders stoop as she curls in on herself.

CHORUS 2. Harry isn't getting out much.

CHORUS 1. But if you are to find her anywhere, it'll be here –
A high hill in Greenwich, the winding Thames stretched out before her,
Repeating an action she first learnt as a child,
And has since come to place altogether too much significance in –
She closes her eyes and straddles the Meridian Line –
Longitude zero: the place from which everything starts.

CHORUS.
  A TALL SHIP
  AND A FAIR BREEZE
  AND A CLEAR VIEW
  AND A CALM SEA
  AND IT'S EASY, EASY

CHORUS 1. And it sounds silly, but it brings her such comfort,
  this imaginary marker that races all the way around the
  world, only existing because somebody says it does, because
  all journeys must start somewhere.

CHORUS.
  A TALL SHIP
  AND A HIGH TIDE
  AND A WHITE SAIL
  AND A BLUE SKY
  AND IT'S EASY, EASY

CHORUS 1. And there is a song Harry has been trying to
  remember – a song from her childhood, she thinks – about
  a woman who has spent her entire life at sea, and dreams
  every night of walking on dry land.

CHORUS.
  A WESTERN WIND AND A PROW OF GOLD
  AND THE WATERS PART BEFORE ME

CHORUS 1. It's only recently she's realised who the woman is.
  She catches glimpses of her sometimes
  Half-hidden in fugged-up bus windows
  Or bathroom mirrors before the bulb reaches full glow.
  She's in there, but she never lingers long.

CHORUS.
  TALL SHIP, FAIR BREEZE, CLEAR VIEW, CALM SEAS
  WATERS PART BEFORE ME

CHORUS 1. Harry pushes her shoulders back and leans into
  the wind.

CHORUS.
  TALL SHIP, HIGH TIDE, WHITE SAIL, BLUE SKIES
  WATERS PART BEFORE ME

CHORUS 1. She has such a long journey ahead of her.
    The ocean is vast, but there must be some way across it.
    She imagines the eddies carrying her upwards,
    Making her featherweight.
    She is waiting for a storm
    To be struck by lightning while airborne
    And transformed in that moment,
    Wings exploding from shoulderblades,
    Or her whole body bursting into light,
    A spray of sparks that scatter across the stars.

Music stops.

9.

JO *is alone. She maybe wears a large backpack.*

JO. And there are some things, some things, and you can do as much forward-planning as you like, consult the stars or seek medical guidance, take your pills and say your prayers, but no way of entirely guaranteeing you won't start your period on the first day of the Inca Trail. You can't know that for sure. You can't really prepare for the altitude, as you come to appreciate that 'breathtaking' isn't always a metaphorical term. You can't fully wrap your head around it until you're there – the sky, the scale, the air, the exhilaration and the sheer exertion of the climb. Relax – thousands of people do this. Hundreds of thousands over hundreds of years. You are youngish. You are in decent shape. You are Beyoncé in hiking boots, more or less. Just keep putting one foot in front of the other, and you'll be fine.

It's day three of four when you fall – an undignified tumble arse over tit and a gash of about six inches up your left shin – it isn't deep, but it bleeds profusely. It's the heat, you see. The guides are great – you're swabbed and bandaged – water, snack, rest – a little sit, you'll be right as rain. And so you sit, gazing out at this unfamiliar and unreasonably beautiful landscape, and maybe it's the shock, or the heat, or the blood-loss, but suddenly the thought hits you that you're now so successfully unplugged, so thoroughly in control of your own destiny, that no one you know could place you within a hundred-mile radius. And you're not really in pain any more, but now you're crying, crying, it's so embarrassing but you're crying these big, fat, ugly, snotty tears, and it's at this moment – because of course it is – that the most unreasonably beautiful woman you have ever seen turns the corner – this thirty-something gazelle goddess, long-limbed and effortless. You're hoping she won't notice you, or just mistake you for some lesser-spotted Peruvian mountain toad, but no, she sees you, she heads over and says –

GABBY *appears.*

GABBY. Are you okay?

JO. And for some reason the only words that leave your mouth are 'I've let Beyoncé down.'

GABBY. I'm sorry?

JO. No, I'm sorry – I'm fine.

GABBY. Did you fall?

JO. Yeah, just a…

GABBY *giggles.* JO *looks confused.*

GABBY. Sorry, sorry. (*She giggles again.*) I just… I thought of the line – 'Did it hurt, when you fell from heaven?', but you actually just fell over, so… (*Laughs.*) Sorry. That isn't funny. I'm Gabby.

JO. Jo.

GABBY. Do you want a brownie?

JO. They gave me an energy bar.

GABBY. Yeah, but do you want a pot brownie?

JO. Oh.

GABBY. They're good. I'm having the best time.
(*A conspiratorial whisper.*) You don't look like you're
having the best time.

JO. Yeah. Yeah, fuck it. Why not?

Now GABBY *and* JO *are telling their story to us/the*
CHORUS.

GABBY. And we walk the final day together.

JO. A solid twenty-four hours together.

GABBY. We swap battle scars and life stories,
Pet peeves and political allegiances
We never leave each other's side
We hold hands and get high,
Pouring scorn on all those who take life so seriously.

JO. Gabby has a terrible tattoo of her own.

GABBY. Shut up!

JO. She does!

GABBY. It's true, I do.

JO. A snake and an apple on her ankle –
A memento of the woman who opened her eyes and broke
her heart –

GABBY. Oh shut up!

JO. Although actually it looks more like a worm.

GABBY. Right, I'm going.

JO. No, come back!

CHORUS 4. Gabby is luminous.

CHORUS 2. Gabby is a laugh.

CHORUS 3. Gabby, believe it or not, lives in Brighton –

CHORUS 1. Glimpses the sea from her attic bedroom.

GABBY (*to* JO). You should come see it.

JO. Yeah?

GABBY. The water's lovely.

CHORUS 4. And it is quite the thing
   Quite a special thing
   To kiss someone goodbye at the foot of the mountain.
   Too special to leave things there.

Music starts creeping in.

CHORUS.
   OPEN ME UP
   I'M NOT AFRAID
   YOU ARE THE ONE
   I'VE BEEN WAITING FOR…

CHORUS 4. And so despite barely having known each other for
   a day

CHORUS 1. Or perhaps because of this

CHORUS 3. A little over a week later Jo finds herself taking
   a train to the seaside

CHORUS 2. And Gabby takes her dancing.

Music swells joyously.

CHORUS.
   I, I WILL CLIMB MOUNTAINS WITH YOU
   I WILL MOVE MOUNTAINS FOR YOU
   I WILL CARVE OUT A NEW WORLD FOR US
   A NEW WORLD FOR US

   PLANT YOUR FLAG IN ME

Music continues. JO *and* GABBY *are almost shouting
over it.*

JO. This is her favourite spot –
    Strong drinks and clean lines –
    Electro-chic design that makes me feel like I'm stuck inside
    an iPhone –

GABBY. Be nice.

JO. Gabby is a Futurist, decked out in space-age metallics
    And we dance like robots
    Like fucking fibre-optic cyborgs played by Janelle Monáe.

GABBY. Do you hate it?

JO. No. I don't hate it.

GABBY. And for the first time in such a long time
    Tomorrow feels like a place Jo wants to visit,
    And she tears towards it at lightspeed.

CHORUS.
    I, I WILL FIGHT ARMIES FOR YOU
    FOR I AM AN ARMY WITH YOU
    I WILL CONQUER A NEW WORLD FOR US
    A NEW WORLD FOR US

    PLANT YOUR FLAG IN ME

JO. And there are chips on the beach

GABBY. And saltwater kisses

JO. And a bed with a glimpse of the sea

GABBY. And this new-and-improved Jo
    Finally free to feel her own feelings
    Declares –

JO (*to* GABBY.) This is it – this is what I've been missing.

    JO *and* GABBY *join in with the ending. Raucous drunken
    karaoke style.*

CHORUS.
    THE WORLD IS FUCKED
    I WILL CLING TO YOU
    THE WORLD IS FUCKED

LET ME CLING TO YOU
THE WORLD IS FUCKED
LET ME BUILD UP A NEW WORLD WITH YOU
A NEW WORLD WITH YOU

PLANT YOUR FLAG IN ME
PLANT YOUR FLAG IN ME

Song ends. Into –

10.

LILY *is with* HARRY. *She has just learnt about Jo and Gabby.*

LILY. I just thought you should know.

HARRY. Yeah.

LILY. She hadn't said anything?

HARRY. We're having a bit of a break from talking. (*Beat.*) Is it serious, do you think? Is it… Is it just sex, or…?

LILY. I don't know.

HARRY. Have you met her? You said 'Gabby', didn't you? She's a – ?

LILY. Yeah. (*Beat.*) They're not going to be there tonight. A lot of us will be, though – me and Cassie and a bunch more.

HARRY. Yeah.

LILY. You don't have to come, but you're a part of this now.

LILY *gives* HARRY *a little squeeze and moves aside. Other* CHORUS FRIENDS *join her.*

LEIGH. She won't come.

LILY. She said she'd try.

LEIGH. She won't. She doesn't get it.

Underscore starts to creep in.

CHORUS 3. Harry never comes. She's always invited –
Shopping trips, spa days and movie nights,
Any opportunity to be one-of-the-girls.

CHORUS 2. Tonight's different though.
Tonight we're marching.

CHORUS 4. Marching because another woman has died,
Another woman *killed*,
Another woman didn't make it home
And so rather than sit alone with our rage and our sorrow
We come to stand together.
Light a candle, when we want to set the whole world on fire.

EVE *sends* HARRY *a message.*

EVE. Are you okay?

HARRY. Yeah, fine.

EVE. You promise?

CHORUS 4. But Harry won't stand beside us
Because she's not sure she's allowed
Because this seems sacred, almost – beyond her reach
Because shoulder-to-shoulder her shoulders are too broad
Footsteps fall too heavy
Her long shadow is a knife blade and she doesn't know how
to sheathe it.

EVE (*to* HARRY). We'll look after you.

CHORUS 4. And so instead, at home in the dark,
Sitting alone with her rage and her sorrow
She thinks of the stories Jo would tell her –
Of the colleague who couldn't be dissuaded,
The stranger on the Tube, the drunk who followed her home,
The way her whole body would sometimes sag with the
weight of it,
Of simply being a woman in this world – of what that entails.
And Jesus, who would opt in to all of that?
But there is something else now

A memory she had deeply boxed away
From the worst times, when all the worst things were said.

Music cuts out. JO *appears. She and* HARRY *are in the middle of an argument.*

JO. It doesn't work like that.

HARRY. I know, but –

JO. No, you don't – you don't understand what it's like to –

HARRY. I'm just saying because, because you do, because historically you have dated women – predominantly dated –

JO. It isn't the same.

HARRY. I'm just saying if you were one hundred per cent straight –

JO. See! You don't think it should make a difference! But women are different! Dating a woman is different! This affects me, okay?

HARRY. I know.

JO. You don't! And you don't get to dictate… You were the same with kids – making the same arguments over and over, trying to wear me down.

HARRY. That's not… I respected –

JO. Then respect me now.

HARRY. I'm only asking that we try.

JO. I've tried!

HARRY. No, but you can't know until… It's such early days – for me, for us, for everything, so if me right now… *I* don't like how I am right now, but –

JO. Harry –

HARRY. Once I get – *if* I go on hormones, that can… People transform, they really –

JO. It's not about that.

HARRY. I know it's a lot. It's an adjustment.

JO. It's more than… It's *ten years*! Ten years I knew you as
a man, as – fuck – as one of the only decent men I ever…
And now you want me to just… You want me to call you
a woman, fine. I can do that. I will respect you, defend you,
fight your corner, but you can't force me into… And this
fixation, this obsession with me liking women –

HARRY. I wasn't –

JO. It doesn't mean *all* women, okay.

> *A beat, then the flashback ends.* JO *goes,* CHORUS *return.*
> *Underscore restarts.*

CHORUS 3. So there it is: Not all women
  Harry is different
  And there are some things she will never truly understand.
  Things like tonight.
  Because she has – of course she has –
  She's been abused, harassed,
  Confronted at handbasins
  And chased off housing estates,
  But it's not the same.
  She gets 'What the fuck is that?'
  And 'Did you see the state?'
  And 'You shouldn't be in here'
  And other far more unrepeatable…
  But it isn't for being a woman –
  It's for *not* being a woman – that's the point.
  That's why she can't face us
  She doesn't count, so she can't stand and be counted.

EVE (*getting a text message*). She isn't coming.

CHORUS 3. Harry hangs up her new winter coat
  Still yet to be worn outside.
  Bolts the door. Takes out her make-up wipes.
  Wonders what it means, to have never had that.
  Wonders what it'll mean, when she finally does.

CHORUS 4. Something to look forward to then.

CHORUS 3. And the truth of the thought catches in her throat
     Because yes, she is, just a little bit –
     Looking forward to it.
     Like it might prove something.

CHORUS 4. And what real woman could ever think like that?

Music swells and cuts out.

11.

JO *and* GABBY *are with Gabby's friends,* GAYLE, ASH *and*
MAYA. *Suddenly cheerful again.*

MAYA. On top of a mountain?

GABBY. On top of a motherfucking mountain.

CHORUS 2. Jo is making new friends. Gabby's friends.

MAYA. That is the most lesbian shit I've ever heard.

CHORUS 2. The sort she always hoped she'd have,
     Cool and queer and effortlessly interesting.

ASH. Nice story for the grandkids.

JO. Whose grandkids?

CHORUS 2. Ignore that.

MAYA. Whose do you think?

CHORUS 2. Don't blow this.

GAYLE (*to* JO). And you were married before?

JO (*slightly thrown*). Um, yeah.

GABBY (*to* GAYLE) What's wrong with you? Why would you
     ask about that?

MAYA. For how long?

JO. God. Almost five years.

ASH. I couldn't be with a man for five hours.

GAYLE. I think my record is five minutes.

JO. Um, no, Harry isn't...

ASH. Isn't what?

JO. A man. Harry's not a man.

MAYA. Oh, sorry – I thought Gabby said –

GABBY. I... (*To* JO.) Okay, it's your ex.

JO. She's not. She's... Don't say that.

GABBY. Sorry.

GAYLE. I'm confused. Why're you being weird?

JO. I'm not. Harry is a woman. She... She hadn't started living as a woman when we were together, but –

ASH (*laughs*). Oh shit! You mean – ?

JO. She's trans, yeah.

ASH. Fuck! Okay, well congrats on escaping that shitshow.

MAYA (*to* JO). Ignore her – we all do.

GABBY. Maybe we talk about something else, yeah?

This moment disappears. JO *stays.*

CHORUS 2. It's fine.
   People are entitled to their own opinions, aren't they?
   Don't let it take away from anything
   Not from this head-over-heels and pinch-me-quick,
   The way Gabby fills her head with music,
   Each smile putting her right back on top of the mountain.

GABBY. I'm sorry about them. Are you mad at me?

CHORUS 4. How could she be?
   Gabby steals kisses at the kitchen sink

When Jo is soapy and defenceless
Incapable of denying her mountain goddess anything,
including –

GABBY. You can't just quit your job.

JO. Why not? I hate my job.

GABBY. So join the club. Be a grown-up.

CHORUS 3. Which is fine as well – she can do that –
And maybe she's not quite as unplugged as she'd once planned
But with Gabby it's different – nothing like before
Her last chance, her missing piece,
Her constant comrade against the robot hordes.
She willingly cedes territory –
A toothbrush, a shelf, a drawer,
Her doorkey, her heart, her all.
Her city walls crumble with a touch –

GABBY (*sings softly*).
PLANT YOUR FLAG IN ME
PLANT YOUR FLAG IN ME

CHORUS 2. And soon two lives are utterly intertwined:
Jo and Gabby – Jobby, as we affectionately come to know
them –
One single semi-domesticated entity
And then, on a soggy summit somewhere in Snowdonia
Gabby stages a pratfall and hauls herself up onto one knee –

GABBY. Marry me.

JO. Fuck off.

GABBY. I mean it. Marry me.

JO. Are you serious?

GABBY. Did you just tell me to fuck off?

JO. Sorry.

GABBY. Marry me. That's it – three times of asking is my
limit.

JO (*with three kisses*). Yes. Yes. Yes.

CHORUS 2. And there is cake and fizz and a surprise party
  Where we take it upon ourselves to dress as sexy nuns
  And bellow –

CHORUS. 'Climb every mountain!'

CHORUS 2. And Jo is taking all of this in her stride.

JO (*as a toast*). Forever isn't so scary when it's with the right
  person.

CHORUS 2. And now there's a wedding to plan, and a joint
  bank account,
  And an ever-so-slightly tense conversation about soft
  furnishings,
  And everything is going *so* fast –

  A little glitch/flicker and HARRY *is there too. The world
  slows down.*

CHORUS 1. And Jo pauses just long enough to write a long
  letter to the person who was once her person.

  JO *and* HARRY *are looking at each other.* HARRY *holds
  a letter.*

JO. 'Because I wanted you to hear this from me.'

CHORUS 1. And –

JO. 'I hope you're – '

CHORUS 1. And –

JO. 'I don't know if – '

CHORUS 1. And –

JO. 'Whenever you're ready to – '

CHORUS 1. Harry writes a dozen replies, all unsent,
  Before instructing a solicitor not to draw anything out
  Signs whatever's put in front of her.
  So that's that then.

HARRY *goes.*

CHORUS 2. And Jo isn't out of the woods just yet.
There's still another conversation she must have –
One she's been avoiding.
The one concession she's still not prepared to make.
And yet –

GABBY *takes* HARRY*'s spot.*

GABBY. I thought you knew how I felt.

JO. I –

GABBY. I thought you understood. (*Beat.*) I did tell you. I was upfront.

CHORUS 2. She was, but the love-struck never listen.
How could she hear anything over all that music?

GABBY. Couldn't imagine a life without children.

JO. Yeah.

GABBY. Not… It doesn't have to be tomorrow, but –

JO. Yeah.

GABBY. And it wouldn't have to change everything.

JO. I think it would.

GABBY. Not everything. Not between us. It wouldn't change who we are.

JO. But it would.

GABBY. And I think we'd be brilliant – you'd be brilliant.

JO. That's not…

GABBY. I've done the numbers – if we budget properly –

JO. You're not listening. I've been through this before.

GABBY (*genuinely confused*). No we haven't.

JO. No, not with you, but...

GABBY. I'd carry it – I'd want to do that – all you have to do is be there with me. And I do want you – only you, no one else – but if you won't... If I never do this and it's because of you, I'll just end up resenting you forever, so –

JO. So it's an ultimatum?

GABBY. Don't say it like that. It's an adventure. Fuck. It's what we're here for.

CHORUS 2. And with Gabby it's different.

JO. Is it?

GABBY. Isn't it? You know it is.

> THE WORLD IS FUCKED
> LET ME BUILD UP A NEW WORLD WITH YOU
> A NEW WORLD WITH YOU

12.

We hear the giggle of a small child. HARRY *is having a video-call with* ELAINE *and* BETH, *Harry's sister.*

ELAINE. Can you see us all?

HARRY. Just about. Is that Jessie somewhere?

BETH (*coming into shot*). Somewhere – running around, being a madam.

HARRY. Not too jet-lagged then?

BETH. No, apparently not. I've raised a terrorist. (*Off.*) Yes, I am talking about you. (*Back to* HARRY.) You don't want her, do you?

HARRY. Got my hands pretty full, actually.

BETH. Yeah, yeah. (*Off.*) Uncle Harry's too smart to have kids.

HARRY *winces, but doesn't contradict her.*

You have to see my bridesmaid's dress – it's horrific.

ELAINE (*chastising*). Be nice!

BETH. It's lime-green! It's a human rights violation.

HARRY. You're a bridesmaid?

BETH. Yeah, all the girls are. Jessie gets to be a flower girl too. Very cute.

HARRY. Wow.

ELAINE (*to* HARRY). And have you actually booked your flights yet?

HARRY. Not quite. I'm getting there.

BETH. Mum said something about your passport?

HARRY. Yeah, yeah, almost sorted, I just need this doctor's letter first.

BETH. Doctor's – why?

HARRY. Oh, just because… admin bullshit, but I got a cancellation slot, and because I've been waiting so long already, just as long as I can prove I've been living as… well, as *me* for over a year they should just tick a box, and –

BETH. What, a year as…? Has it been that long?

HARRY. Yeah. Quite a bit longer, actually. Anyway…

ELAINE. I thought this was done with. In your email you said –

HARRY. It should be. Hopefully after this.

BETH. I still can't believe you skipped out on Bermuda.

HARRY. It wasn't my specialism anyway. Richard was leading it –

BETH. Ooh, is he the one we hate?

HARRY. Yeah, that's him.

BETH. God I remember that time when… (*Distracting herself, calling off.*) No. Put it down. Put it down. (*To others.*) Sorry. I've got to deal with this. (*To* HARRY.) Love you!

BETH *goes.*

HARRY (*after her*). Love you! (*To* ELAINE.) Never stops, does it?

ELAINE. So this passport – you're still trying to – ?

HARRY. It's happening – it is – I'm on top of it.

ELAINE. Yes, but –

HARRY. Flying is still… You know I did look into boats, actually. I won't – takes forever, costs a fortune – but I do like the idea of… I think I've just been spending too much time in Greenwich. Do you remember the Meridian Line – the place where everything starts?

ELAINE (*genuinely thrown*). What?

HARRY. Did you used to sing us a song about a woman on a ship? It's something I've had going round my head –

ELAINE. Harry – the wedding.

HARRY. Yes – I'm going to be there, I promise. Customs will be terrifying, but –

ELAINE. Don't pack any explosives and you'll be fine.

HARRY. Yeah, no, it's just… You hear a lot about… people get hassled, harassed, or you can set off, um, the body scanners, because they register abnormalities – what they consider to be bodily abnormalities based on…

ELAINE. Yes, but not if…

HARRY. Not if what?

ELAINE. If you just... If you don't come as Harriet. If you just come as... If you use the passport you have already, avoid all this unnecessary...

HARRY. It isn't –

ELAINE. We talked about this – we agreed the easiest thing –

HARRY. No –

ELAINE. As you haven't started anything yet, anything medical... Of course we all want you here, but...

HARRY. But what?

ELAINE. But it's the whole family – not just ours, Michael's whole family.

HARRY. Yes?

ELAINE. You know what I'm trying to say.

HARRY. No I don't.

ELAINE. You shouldn't be a distraction. We've discussed it and I have to say I agree. He likes you – he's always liked you – but it's Rachel's day – the focus should be on her.

HARRY. What do you think I'm going to do?

ELAINE. And I really don't see why for one day – or for one trip, even, when I'm trying to make a good impression – why it would be so impossible to –

HARRY. To pretend nothing's changed?

ELAINE. To put on a suit you've worn a dozen times before.

HARRY. Right.

ELAINE. To come as you are. I told you. I thought when we spoke before you understood.

HARRY. I didn't. I didn't understand that, no.

ELAINE. Not everything is about you, sweetheart. I can't just let you hijack his daughter's wedding for your... I will love you regardless, whatever you're wearing, but you know it's not for everyone.

HARRY. Yeah. I should… That's fine. It's better if I stay here. Work is busy, and –

ELAINE. That's not what I'm asking.

HARRY. I can't.

ELAINE. Harry –

HARRY (*fighting to remain calm*). No, I actually can't. Because they… if you want help, want treatment, they need proof – proof that you've been living as… as yourself, that you are committed and consistent and socialised in… They ask you – they specifically ask you if there's anyone you're not out to, so if I turn up in front of everyone like… If I pretend, even if I wanted to, and I don't want to. It's been over a year, Mum. I don't have a suit.

ELAINE. Michael's calling. We can talk about this again later. Stay safe.

She hangs up. Music plays.

CHORUS 1. And so there is to be no maiden voyage. No flight. Not yet.

CHORUS.
    A TALL SHIP

HARRY. It's better actually.

CHORUS.
    AND A FAIR BREEZE

HARRY. Bad for the planet anyway.

CHORUS.
    A CLEAR VIEW

HARRY. It's not important.

CHORUS.
    AND A CALM SEA

CHORUS 1. And Harry is hanging on by a thread sometimes
Her sense of self is such a fragile thing
A fucking gossamer construction that makes her want to weep
At the absurdity of what she's asking –
'Clap, children, to show you believe in fairies'
See me as what I am.
See me as I see me.

CHORUS.
AND IT'S EASY
IT SHOULD BE EASY

CHORUS 1. But still, the world doesn't end.
Instead, Harry has an appointment to attend –
And she sweats and frets and fidgets
Repaints her nails, lays out half a dozen outfits
Because she's heard stories –

EVE. What sort of stories?

HARRY. Oh, just about what they're looking for.

EVE. Right.

HARRY. Make-up, hair, that sort of thing.

EVE. Really?

HARRY. This one woman I heard about, she got denied treatment
the first time round because she turned up wearing jeans.

EVE. What?

HARRY. Yeah. Jeans aren't feminine enough, apparently. So
how do I look?

EVE. Honestly? Like a 1950s housewife.

HARRY. Good. I think that's good.

EVE. Okay, then good luck.

CHORUS.
TALL SHIP, FAIR BREEZE, CLEAR VIEW, CALM SEA
WATERS PART BEFORE ME

Into –

13.

JO *and* GABBY *are with another* DOCTOR. *A bomb has just been dropped.*

GABBY. I don't understand.

DOCTOR 2. And you should absolutely take some time to process this.

GABBY. No, I don't understand. I do everything right. I don't smoke. I work out. I'm in the... the...

DOCTOR 2. Yes.

GABBY. Last year I was told – only last year... You'll have to do the tests again.

DOCTOR 2. I'm very sorry.

GABBY. No, don't be sorry, just do them again. It's a mistake.

DOCTOR 2. There's not a great deal more we can ascertain here. In cases of Uterine Factor Infertility the options are a little more limited, but –

GABBY. Then we'll go somewhere else. (*To* JO.) Come on.

JO. It'll be okay, I promise.

GABBY. How? How will it...? Now you've got what you wanted?

JO. That's not –

DOCTOR 2. If you'd like to schedule an appointment with –

GABBY. No, I just want to go. Let's go. I want to... to... I have to...

GABBY *stumbles and almost falls.* JO *catches her.*

JO. Hey – hey – I've got you –

GABBY. Get off me!

JO *tries to steady* GABBY *then turns to the* DOCTOR. *She speaks before she knows what she's saying.*

JO. What if you tested me?

GABBY. What?

JO. Just to... I'm not promising – and maybe I can't either – but we could...

GABBY. But...

JO. Just to, um, to get the information – to know where we stand?

DOCTOR 2. We could certainly arrange that.

GABBY (*to* JO). You'd do that?

JO speaks her thoughts out loud – a stream of consciousness – an out-of-body experience.

JO. And I can't. I'm saying yes but I can't. Yes to testing – only testing – but I can't, and her eyes, something in her eyes keeps... so I'm saying yes, I keep saying yes, even though I can't, I know I can't, because I can't I can't I can't I can't lose her. Not her. Not this one. So what else can I do?

Music plays. A delicate reprise.

CHORUS.
I, I WOULD MOVE MOUNTAINS FOR YOU
I WILL MOVE MOUNTAINS WITH YOU
I'LL LAY CLAIM TO A NEW WORLD FOR US
A NEW WORLD FOR US

GABBY *looks up at* JO. *The scene disappears.*

CHORUS 3. Gabby seems to transform overnight into an entirely different person
Someone with binders and pamphlets and ovulation charts.
Someone who makes the unilateral decision to replace their home bar with a DIY smoothie station:

GABBY (*handing* JO *a glass*). Drink this.

JO. What is it?

GABBY. You don't want to know. Bottoms up.

CHORUS 3. Someone who says things like –

GABBY (*to* JO). You know your maternity package is pretty great actually – it's a good thing you stuck around.

JO. And I see the breadth of eternity stretching out before me

CHORUS. PLANT YOUR FLAG IN ME

JO. A vanishingly small window through which to escape.

CHORUS. PLANT YOUR FLAG IN ME

CHORUS 4. And she watches as it closes.

Music shifts.

14.

CHORUS 1. And Harry attends an appointment that proves blissfully anticlimactic.
She is heard. She is seen. She is handled with sympathetic efficiency.
Boxes are ticked, and details will be in the post.
She is on a pathway now. Wheels are in motion.

CHORUS 4. And Harry is waiting on a quiet train platform in Kettering
Where she's been attending a conference on biodiversity in cold-water climates
Followed by drinks with an old uni friend
Because she is trying to get out more
She has been trying
And she drank two large glasses of red wine
And talked passionately about rare breeds of algae
And it was good. It was almost normal. It was a small victory.
And it's approaching eleven p.m. when off another train comes an older gent,

Neat beard, kind eyes,
Who grins at her as he passes, and says –

A MAN *appears next to* HARRY. *Music stops.*

MAN. Hi.

HARRY. Hi?

CHORUS 4. And she smiles, and thinks it slightly strange
Wonders if she knows him
And the wine is making her recollection hazy,
But no, he's just friendly, that's all.
Except he comes back.
He passes her, then doubles back
Lingers once the other passengers have drifted away
Offers up –

MAN. I like your coat.

CHORUS 4. And it is a nice coat. Her nice winter coat, finally
being worn.
She has been trying.
So she smiles again, thanks him, blushes, this is all…

MAN. Aren't you a lovely specimen?

CHORUS 4. And that's… okay. It doesn't feel okay,
But then she doesn't know the rules of this game,
Never learnt it when we all did.
He moves a step closer
Feels the fabric of her sleeve
And then somehow, somehow he has her hand –

MAN. Do you do the tango?

HARRY. I'm sorry?

MAN. I'd like to go dancing with you.

CHORUS 4. Which strikes her as almost sweet, old-fashioned
somehow,
But his grip is firm. He's not letting go.
She glances over his shoulder and can see they're essentially
alone.

MAN. I bet you're a great dancer.

HARRY. No, two left feet, honestly.

CHORUS 4. Trying to keep things friendly, light,
    Her voice light, her secrets safe –

MAN. No, just look at you.
    I bet you're a firecracker.
    I bet you're red-hot.

HARRY. No –

CHORUS 4. Head tilt, deflecting laugh –

HARRY. Cold fish, me.

MAN. No. No, you're red-hot, I know you are.

CHORUS 4. And he smiles as his grip tightens, almost
    imperceptibly.

MAN. So when are we going dancing?

HARRY. I –

CHORUS 4. And here it is – her train is pulling in.

HARRY. I'm sorry, this is me.

MAN. You could take me home with you.

HARRY. I'm sorry –

CHORUS 4. Why is she apologising?

HARRY. But my boyfriend will be waiting.

MAN/CHORUS 4. Liar.

CHORUS 4. Why did she say that?

HARRY. Sorry.

CHORUS 4. Why does she keep saying that?

HARRY. Have a nice night.

CHORUS 4. And with just a little tug her hand is hers again,
    Still forcing a smile –
    Why is she still smiling?
    And while she's walking away she hears

MAN. You should take my number.

CHORUS 4. Breathe.

MAN. Cunt.

    Music starts.

CHORUS 4. She doesn't look back.
    Steps onto the train
    And she is shaking.
    Praying he doesn't follow
    And he doesn't
    But she is still shaking
    Finds a seat and is still shaking
    Because of how he looked at her,
    Violating and validating,
    In some shameful, ugly way
    And there was no victory in it, none at all.

CHORUS 2. It was nothing.

CHORUS 4. This was her first time.

CHORUS 2. And it was nothing – she knows that.

CHORUS 1. She's stupid.

CHORUS 2. She handled it badly.

CHORUS 4. She can still feel the clammy pressure of his grip,
    Indentations of each finger
    Still shaking
    Her first time.
    So this is what it feels like.

CHORUS 2. And can she really do this? A lifetime of it?
    Even if she ever gets to where she's going –
    Will it always be like this?

CHORUS 1. But there is no time to question,
Because when she arrives home a letter is waiting for her,
The crucial part of which reads:

DOCTOR 3. 'I would regard the patient as fitting the ICD-ten
diagnostic criteria for F sixty-four point zero male to female
transsexualism.'

CHORUS 1. Which makes her toes curl, and her skin itch, and
equally:

DOCTOR 3. 'She presented in a straightforwardly female role,
wearing a floral top and with painted nails'

CHORUS 1. And most importantly of all –

DOCTOR 3. 'There are, in my opinion, no contraindications to
commencing hormone therapy. I believe she will have a good
outcome from oestrogen.'

CHORUS 4. And a form for her to fill out – a legal disclaimer –

HARRY. 'The patient understands that the proposed treatment
will likely lead to permanent infertility.'

JO *returns*.

CHORUS 2. And there are blood tests, and further blood tests,
Herbal supplements and vitamin D prescriptions,
And private clinics in tasteful shades of sage and oatmeal
That make Jo feel like she's in Waitrose
Legs splayed in what might as well be the chilled-goods aisle
Stuffed with needles and wires and readings, so far from
unplugged.

CHORUS 1. And Harry leans into the wind on a high hill in
Greenwich.

CHORUS 3. Jo closes her eyes and tries to picture herself back
on top of the mountain.

CHORUS 2. Trying to imagine the unimaginable.

CHORUS 4. Waiting for news that the world has changed.

A shift in the music. JO and HARRY *stand facing each other, as if looking in a mirror.*

HARRY. And she stands

JO. In front of the long mirror

HARRY. Staring, scrutinising.

JO. Eyes trying to pierce her skin

HARRY. Hands searching for growth –

JO. Lumps –

HARRY. Clues –

JO. Wondering what she might be capable of.

HARRY. Within four-to-six weeks you may experience an itching or a soreness.

JO. At four weeks your child is the size of a poppy seed.

HARRY. Increased sensitivity

JO. At six weeks a sweet pea

HARRY. As the breast buds begin to form

JO. Nine weeks a green olive

HARRY. Two solid, olive-sized lumps

JO. Why a *green* olive?

HARRY. That may be tender and sensitive.

JO. Twelve weeks, a plum

HARRY. Then two golf balls

JO. Peach, lemon, orange, avocado

HARRY. The bud forms before the rest of the breast.

JO. Always the most middle-class foods.

HARRY. It is possible to experience lactation.

JO. Never a… a Kinder Egg, or a Turkey Twizzler.

HARRY. This is not necessarily a cause for concern, but you should consult your doctor.

JO. At week twenty you reach banana.

HARRY. The milk ducts begin to develop at Tanner Stage Two.

JO. Which seems implausible, when you think of the dimensions.

HARRY. There are five stages of the Tanner Scale, stage five representing full adult development.

JO. Cravings are normal. Pain is normal.

HARRY. You are unlikely to reach stage five.

JO. It is not uncommon to feel anxious or overwhelmed.

HARRY. You may also experience emotional changes.

JO. No two cases are alike.

CHORUS 1. And Harry knows in that moment
The only thing more terrifying than going forward
Is staying where she is.

JO (*calling off*). Gabby!

CHORUS 1. And soon Harry is holding another piece of paper –
A thin green slip that she tries not to crumple in her fist
A thin green slip that acquires her a box of small white pills.

JO (*still calling off*). Gabby! Get in here!

CHORUS 4. And Jo finds herself staring down the barrel of two pink lines.

GABBY *joins* JO.

GABBY. You're sure?

JO. I need to call my mum.

GABBY. But you're sure?

JO. Is it too soon?

GABBY. I'm going to call everyone.

JO. It's ringing. Jesus.

GABBY. I love you.

JO. Fuck. Fuck. Fuck.

GABBY. Wine? Should we – ? No, you can't. You are
a goddess.

JO. Just breathe.

GABBY. Sorry, yeah.

JO. It's okay. This is the right thing, isn't it?

CHORUS 2. And Harry lies on her back
Adrift on the endless ocean
In the centre of the king-sized bed she used to share,
And up until this night
Had been keeping to her old side –
As if she was still saving a place
Still waiting for Jo to slip back under the covers
And press her cold feet against Harry's warm flesh
But now she stretches out
Starfishing towards its corners
Attempting to reclaim every inch.

JO. And she stands in front of the long mirror.

HARRY. Lost in the long mirror

JO. And on good days

HARRY. Even if it's too early

JO. Even if she can't see it yet

HARRY. She knows something is changing.

JO. Yes.

HARRY. Yes.

JO/HARRY (*together*). Yes.

Music ends.

End of Act One.

ACT TWO

1.

We are not in the same place we left off. HARRY *and* JO *are still with us, in shadow/partially obscured, but now find themselves in some kind of parallel world/alternate reality/fever dream. Neither is entirely human here, but we have to look closely to tell.* JO *is in that uncanny valley of robotics, slightly too smooth and too clean in her movements to be flesh and blood. She also now has some kind of artificial prosthetic belly.* HARRY *is something more animal/monstrous, freshly crawled out of the ocean. Both are quite still. A soundscape underscores as we move between these two realities. In Jo's world, a* TECHNICIAN *welcomes* GABBY.

TECHNICIAN. Ms Parker?

GABBY. Yes?

TECHNICIAN. We have everything set up for you now.

GABBY. Right.

TECHNICIAN. If you want to say hello?

A CAPTAIN *and a* BOSUN *enter on a separate part of the stage. They're from an earlier time. A storm is raging.*

BOSUN. Hold! There's something caught – something moving.

CAPTAIN. Then cut it loose and throw it back in.

BOSUN. No, come look.

They go. The TECHNICIAN *and* GABBY *stand over* JO.

GABBY. And was everything...?

TECHNICIAN. Hmm?

GABBY. It worked? Everything worked?

TECHNICIAN. Yes.

While this continues, the BOSUN *and* CAPTAIN *discover* HARRY *at the back of the stage.*

CAPTAIN. What in God's name?

BOSUN. You see?

Both scenes dovetail.

GABBY. So we can go home?

TECHNICIAN. You can. Just a few forms to fill out first, but –

GABBY. Thank you. Thank you.

CAPTAIN. Is it alive?

BOSUN. I think so. See there – it's twitching.

CAPTAIN. Dead things twitch sometimes.

TECHNICIAN. I know you've been given a lot of information already – you're probably feeling a bit overwhelmed.

GABBY. Yes.

BOSUN. See – it's breathing – trying to –

TECHNICIAN. That's perfectly normal.

CAPTAIN. On its neck – are they…?

BOSUN. I think so. (*Beat.*) What do we do with it?

TECHNICIAN. We have a whole team set up to support you. Anything you've been told today, don't worry about remembering it. We'll be making a house visit later in the week – see how you're getting along.

GABBY. Right.

TECHNICIAN. And we have technicians on-call twenty-four-seven.

A PROFESSOR *has now joined the* BOSUN *and* CAPTAIN.

PROFESSOR. Where did you find it?

BOSUN. South beach – caught in the oyster nets.

PROFESSOR. I see.

TECHNICIAN. Is there anything else you'd like to ask me right now?

GABBY. I don't think so. I think I'd just like to get home.

TECHNICIAN. Of course.

PROFESSOR. A stowaway?

BOSUN. No – look properly.

TECHNICIAN. Let me get those discharge papers now.

The TECHNICIAN *steps away for a moment.*

CAPTAIN (*to the* PROFESSOR). So what will you pay for it?

PROFESSOR. Pay?

CAPTAIN. We shan't part with it for nothing.

PROFESSOR. I don't know who you think I am, but I'm not in the habit of buying women.

BOSUN (*growing more frustrated*). It's not... You're not *looking*. Look at the neck. Look between the fingers, and the toes. Look at its eyes – you look into its eyes and tell me that's human.

PROFESSOR. Unusual, certainly. I'll take care of it.

BOSUN. But –

PROFESSOR. Unless of course you'd rather we contacted the authorities? And what might the charge be – false imprisonment, abduction, trafficking?

CAPTAIN. We're going. (*To the* BOSUN.) I told you we should've thrown it back.

CAPTAIN *and* BOSUN *go.* TECHNICIAN *returns to* GABBY.

TECHNICIAN. I think that's everything. Alright, Mum, shall we get you on your way?

The TECHNICIAN *leads* GABBY *off. A moment of still/ quiet as the* PROFESSOR *is left alone with* HARRY. *We see a little more of her now, wet and dishevelled, still caught up in fishing nets, perhaps. Still recognisably her, but sometimes seen as something monstrous.*

PROFESSOR. Now let's take a proper look at you. Aren't you a lovely specimen?

HARRY looks up at the PROFESSOR, *instinctively drawing back a little. The* PROFESSOR *moves closer, scrutinising her.*

A strange fish. What did they say – fish-woman – frog-woman? (*She chuckles.*) Extraordinary. Can you speak? *Speak?*

The PROFESSOR *mimes speaking.* HARRY *tries to make a sound. Something strange/rattling/rasping comes out. She puts her hand to her throat.*

Don't force it. (*Spotting something on* HARRY's *neck.*) Are they really…? I think you've been through something fairly disastrous. I'll have to run some tests, speak to some colleagues, but I'll get to the bottom of you. Stay there. I'll find you something to eat. You must eat, whatever you are.

The PROFESSOR *goes. Lights shift us into –*

2.

GABBY *has just got robot* JO *home. A polite stiltedness about them.*

GABBY. Right, so come in, come in. Welcome home.

JO. Thank you.

GABBY. What do you…? I made you your own room up – was that stupid? I didn't know what you'd need, what you'd want, but I thought –

JO. That was kind of you.

GABBY. Whatever's best – best for you, best for the…
(*A different thought.*) Can you feel it?

JO. Sorry?

GABBY. The baby – right now – can you – ?

JO. Oh, yes.

GABBY. You can?

JO. Yes.

GABBY. What does it feel like?

JO. As it should. All vital functions stable. They should have given you –

GABBY. No, but what does it *feel* like? Can you tell me?

JO. I'm not sure what you're asking.

GABBY. Right. Sorry.

JO. I'd like to understand.

GABBY. No, ignore me. I'm tired. Are you tired? Stupid question.

JO (*trying to answer helpfully*). I'm heavier.

GABBY. Right.

JO. Slower. They make sure I move slower – it's a precaution – for safety.

GABBY. Oh.

JO. And I think slower too – process slower – there's a lot of new sensory data.

GABBY. Right, yeah.

JO. Full. Does that answer it? I feel very full.

GABBY. Yeah, that's… No, that's clear. Got it. Totally.

JO. I'll work on my similes. I'll find better words for it.

GABBY. Thank you. You're… extraordinary.

JO. Just doing my job.

GABBY. Right.

JO. You said you were tired – if you need to rest –

GABBY. No, no.

JO. I don't need supervision. You can assign me other tasks as well, jobs around the house, or running errands –

GABBY. No, you should rest too.

JO. I don't need to.

GABBY. No, you should – I'd like you to – and I don't think you should be going outside, should you? Not unless… I can take care of everything.

JO. That seems unnecessary.

GABBY. Just to be safe – I think it'd be best if… Because you haven't done this before either, have you?

JO. No.

GABBY. No, so just until we're both settled… Why don't I show you your room – just in case you want it? Why don't you follow me?

GABBY *leads* JO *off.*

3.

The PROFESSOR *has now left and* HARRY *is alone.*
Underscore.

HARRY. I am sore. I am raw. I am bleeding.
 I have been split down the middle.
 Bow-legged and bug-eyed with strange new limbs
 That flop, and ache, and bend in the wrong direction,
 Funny little orphan thing –
 A hermit crab without a shell now fleshy and defenceless,
 Gulls circling above me
 And I thought…
 I thought once I left the water it'd be easy –
 Thought that would be the end of it.
 I would arrive on a tall ship with a prow of burnished gold,
 White sails clean as a fresh-made bed
 And take my first steps unfalteringly
 Not like *this*
 In a storm of scales and nets and squirming here-be-monsters
 I don't recognise this thing that I am now –
 I don't yet know how to control it.
 In the strange dry heat of an uncharted land
 The slashes in the side of my neck heal over completely
 And my new lungs burn with their first full breaths.
 I have arrived.
 I breathe in deep and plant my feet in the earth.

 HARRY *takes a few tentative steps forward. She stumbles,*
 just as the PROFESSOR *returns to help stabilise her. Some*
 time has passed. HARRY*'s language is perhaps slower but*
 precise.

PROFESSOR. You're up?

HARRY. Yes.

PROFESSOR. Good – that's good. Not trying to escape, are you?

HARRY. No.

PROFESSOR. That was a joke. Besides, you still won't get far
 on those. Are you keeping up with your exercises?

HARRY. Yes.

PROFESSOR. Show me.

> HARRY *sits. The* PROFESSOR *examines her lower leg/foot.*

> Healing nicely. Tendons still a little tight. Muscle development strong. Keep at it. (*Beat.*) I have guests coming on Tuesday.

HARRY. I'll be quiet.

PROFESSOR (*cheerfully*). No, no, they're coming for you!

HARRY. Me?

PROFESSOR. Who else? Colleagues – experts – old friends. Dr MacNamara has been studying a baby raised by wolves. Wolves, they're a sort of wild dog, *canis lupus*, and this child exhibits the behavioural patterns of… Oh, and frogs!

HARRY. Frogs?

PROFESSOR. Yes! You remember the frogs – I've told you before. And Professor Cole knows everything there is to know about them. (*Beat.*) Something wrong?

HARRY. No.

PROFESSOR. They might need to take some more samples – blood, urine, maybe tissue. (*Sensing* HARRY*'s discomfort.*) All in a good cause. It's a real honour that they're coming all this way. (*Remembering something.*) Scales! Do you still have scales?

HARRY. No.

PROFESSOR. None? Not by your hairline, or under your breast?

HARRY. All gone now.

PROFESSOR. Never mind, I think I have some stored somewhere. Hands. (*She takes* HARRY*'s hand.*) You need to stop picking, or they'll never heal. Now, you must be hungry.

HARRY. No.

PROFESSOR. No? You need to eat. I know a nice little place not far from here. Very quiet. Private.

HARRY. Can't.

PROFESSOR. Can't what?

HARRY. Last time –

PROFESSOR. That was… unfortunate. You can't blame people for being curious. Wherever you go, people will always…

HARRY. Always?

PROFESSOR. If they've never seen anything like you. Human nature. You'll learn.

HARRY. Please. Don't make me.

PROFESSOR. I thought this was what you wanted. You crawled all the way out of the ocean just to hide away in the dark? (*Beat.*) As you wish. I'll make us something.

The PROFESSOR *goes. Into –*

4.

Robot JO *and* GABBY. GABBY *has a glass of wine.*

GABBY. How is she?

JO. Good.

GABBY. Good?

JO. Very good. Snug as a bug in a rug.

GABBY (*chuckles*). Good. Good simile.

JO. Thank you. (*Beat.*) I have another.

GABBY. Yeah?

JO. It's a warm weight. A pleasant weight. Like a cat sitting on your chest.

GABBY (*surprised*). A cat?

JO. Yes, like a cat you would feel guilty for disturbing. Restrictive, but reassuring. Comforting, in spite of the discomfort. Does that sound right?

GABBY. I wouldn't know.

JO. Sorry.

GABBY. What for? Don't be. Excellent simile. Top marks. Like a cat on your chest? Wow. That's really... You've missed your calling. You should've been a poet. (*Beat.*) How did you feel, when you found out you'd be doing this?

JO. I don't really –

GABBY. You don't really feel, I know, but you're talking about cats and similes and comforting discomfort, so I think we can call bullshit on all of... Because you weren't built to do this, were you?

JO. No. But I was reconfigured for –

GABBY. You were built for sex? (*Beat.*) That's right, isn't it? They told me.

JO. For recreational activities.

GABBY. Right, right.

JO. Rarely sexual acts. Socialisation. Companionship. That's why we get refitted for roles like this – it's about emotional engagement with clients.

GABBY. So that's all I am then – just another John?

JO. No.

GABBY. Yes – hiring your body out for my own ends?

JO. I don't see it like that.

GABBY. And how does that help, exactly? How is it relevant? How does God knows how many years getting fucked by strangers prepare you to carry my child?

JO. It doesn't. I apologise. I explained it badly. Really it just means I can hold a conversation. At least that was the intent.

GABBY. Right.

JO. That isn't who I am any more.

GABBY. No. No, and thank God you've escaped that shitshow. (*Beat*.) Sorry.

JO. You don't have to apologise.

GABBY. No, I'm being rude, dredging up old...

JO. It doesn't upset me.

GABBY. No. I can't actually upset you, can I? Here I am, basically apologising to a toaster and worrying about whether... Fuck! Like I'm actually jealous of... (*Beat*.) Do you remember what it was like – your life before?

JO. My memory doesn't work like yours.

GABBY. No. Do you ever miss it? The... the socialisation?

JO. I'm not set up for recreational sex in my current configuration. There are still some functions I –

GABBY. No! No! Fuck! No, I'm not –

JO. I'd be happy to –

GABBY. No – stop it – forget it. Jesus Christ. (*Beat*.) But she's safe, isn't she? She's good and she's healthy and she's safe – snug as a bug?

JO. She is.

GABBY. So that's alright then. So at least one of us is doing our job. Great.

JO. May I make an observation?

GABBY. Knock yourself out.

JO. I am housing your child. I am holding her here for you. I have been extensively modified to ensure she has the optimal environment in which to thrive. But I am still only a toaster. None of that makes her any less yours.

GABBY. Yes, I know. I know. Thank you. You can go to your room.

5.

A shift. A CHORUS *member appears beside* JO *and* GABBY.

CHORUS 2. And Jo hibernates
Emitting a low-level hum –

Underscore. A slightly unsettling hum.

A low-level purr
From the warm weight of the cat that rests on her stomach
Immovable, invaluable.

And Jo doesn't dream, not exactly,
But she sees things sometimes,
A bedroom with a glimpse of the sea,
And a promise made on top of a mountain –

An autotuned robotic reprise.

CHORUS.
I, I WOULD MOVE MOUNTAINS FOR YOU

CHORUS 2. Where did that come from?

CHORUS.
I WILL MOVE MOUNTAINS WITH YOU

The TECHNICIAN *appears.*

TECHNICIAN. How're the two of you getting on?

CHORUS.
I WILL CARVE OUT A NEW WORLD FOR US
A NEW WORLD FOR US

GABBY. Fine. No, good, fine, great. It's an adjustment.

Robotic music shifts into something more organic. HARRY
appears. The PROFESSOR *is with her – some sort of*
medical presentation. Another CHORUS *member joins.*

CHORUS 1. And somewhere far away the frog-fish-woman
grows steady on her feet.
Her spine straightens. Lungs grow strong.

PROFESSOR (*to an unseen audience*). Friends, today I bring
you something truly remarkable.

CHORUS 1. Learns our language, our manners, our gait,
Until her own actions become indistinguishable.
Almost indistinguishable. Uncanny.

PROFESSOR. You'd almost think her human, if you didn't
know any better. I still have her scales though, for anyone
who wants to see.

The PROFESSOR *moves away, leaving* HARRY *alone.*

GABBY (*to the* TECHNICIAN). It's just… I do worry
sometimes.

TECHNICIAN. About what?

GABBY. About nothing. About everything. About her.

TECHNICIAN. That sounds perfectly normal.

HARRY. I rub aloe into my skin and it softens.
Dry patches fall away in flakes
And when they do, I fantasise about unpeeling myself from
head to toe,
That's what I dream of in the long nights, hot and feverish,
How I would start with that small hole at my centre
And peel my skin back and back and back
Until all my roughness lies like a husk at my feet
And I am glowing, soft and tender and new-born.

TECHNICIAN (*to* GABBY). I think you're doing brilliantly.

The TECHNICIAN *goes.*

CHORUS 2. And Gabby watches her,
  This marvel of engineering,
  This miracle
  This abomination
  And wonders how she could've ever agreed to it,
  To have entrusted something so precious into its care.

GABBY. And sometimes in the long nights, hot and feverish,
  I imagine taking a kitchen knife and freeing her,
  Peeling the synthetic flesh back
  And reclaiming my baby as my own,
  Because surely, surely,
  Surely whatever the experts might say,
  Surely she must fare better in my arms.

JO looks up at GABBY.

JO. Is there anything you need?

GABBY. No, you can rest. We should both rest.

JO and GABBY *go.* HARRY *has taken a coat/long jacket
from somewhere – she starts to dress herself.*

HARRY. With a sharpened flint
  I cut at the tell-tale webbing between my toes
  Each night it grows back, but I persevere
  And soon my feet are a criss-cross mass of scars
  No matter, they will do – they have to.

Underscore pauses. HARRY *is about to go when the*
PROFESSOR *returns. At first glance she mistakes her for
someone else.*

PROFESSOR. I'm sorry, ma'am, can I…? (*Recognising*
HARRY.) Oh, it's you.

HARRY. Yes.

PROFESSOR. I didn't recognise… (*Seeing* HARRY *differently
for the first time.*) Just look at you.

HARRY. I took clothes. I'm sorry.

PROFESSOR. Why? We don't have anything planned today.

HARRY. I have to... To...

PROFESSOR. To what?

HARRY (*finding courage*). Go. I have to leave here.

PROFESSOR. By yourself? (*Beat.*) No. No, it's too dangerous. Without me you'd never... Besides, I still have too many questions about you.

HARRY. So do I – so many questions – and I shan't ever be able to answer them unless I go. (*Beat.*) Will you stop me?

PROFESSOR (*taking some offence*). I'm not... I've only ever... Go on then – go – and good luck to you. (*Now softening, more sincerely.*) Good luck, ma'am. Extraordinary. Safe travels.

The PROFESSOR *shakes* HARRY*'s hand and goes.*

Underscore resumes.

HARRY. I turn my back on the ocean and start to head inland.
Sea becomes estuary becomes river, and I follow it
As the land flattens out and races forest-green towards
a rising sun.
In the distance I see the walls of a great city,
And it glistens with white marble and burnished gold
Like a tall ship promising to bear me off to somewhere better.
I know this place. I have never been here before, but I know it.
Here at last. No time to waste.

HARRY *heads off. Music stops. Into* –

6.

Robot JO, GABBY *and the* TECHNICIAN. *The* TECHNICIAN *is taking some sort of reading from* JO. GABBY *is distressed.*

TECHNICIAN. What happened?

GABBY. She fell.

TECHNICIAN. I see.

GABBY. On a patch of ice. Awful. Ridiculous.

JO. I wasn't –

GABBY. I told her not to. I thought she couldn't. I thought there were precautions – some sort of internal…

TECHNICIAN (*to* JO). You lost your balance?

JO. Some children ran past me. My reactions aren't as fast as they were.

GABBY. Carnage.

JO. No one was hurt.

GABBY. She's a liability.

TECHNICIAN. Everything here seems normal. No damage done.

GABBY. You're sure?

TECHNICIAN. I understand how frightening it must have been for you.

GABBY. Will you tell her – order her – she needs to –

JO. I take precautions.

GABBY (*to the* TECHNICIAN). It was freezing outside. Surely that in itself is –

JO. My core internal temperature is stable at –

GABBY (*still to the* TECHNICIAN). I think there's something wrong with her. She doesn't listen. She thinks she knows better. She ignores me – direct orders.

TECHNICIAN. Really?

The lights flicker. The TECHNICIAN *steps back and for a moment we're with the present-day* JO *and* GABBY *of Act One.*

GABBY. Jo!

JO. What?

GABBY. Are you even listening?

JO. Yes!

GABBY. Where do you go? You just space out, and it's like you –

JO. I'm fine.

GABBY. Fainting in Sainsbury's is not fine.

JO. I didn't faint. I just had a little... a funny spell.

GABBY. A funny spell?

JO. It happens.

GABBY. You shouldn't even be going outside. It's freezing. Look what you're wearing. You can't –

JO. Can you lower your voice around the pregnant lady please?

GABBY. That is my child – *our* child you're carrying.

JO. I'm aware!

GABBY. You need to acknowledge that things are changing –

JO. You said things wouldn't change.

GABBY. You have to –

JO. You actually *promised* me.

GABBY. You are jeopardising... Look at the state of you! You still wear heels. You still run the bath too hot. You still drink – don't deny it – I know you do –

JO. Once in a... The studies say –

GABBY. Oh, so *now* you read the studies – the studies relating to wine.

JO. You still drink!

GABBY. Yes, because I can't... I *can't* so it doesn't matter what I –

JO. I just need to feel human sometimes – feel like my old –

GABBY. Please – I'm begging you –

JO. You don't even look at me like I'm human any more.

GABBY. What does that mean?

JO. You won't touch me. You treat me like I'm some... some...

GABBY. That's not true. That's not –

JO. No?

GABBY. You know I can't do this! This is the one thing that I can't do myself, however much I... So I need you to step up, yeah? I need you to fucking commit and dig deep and...

JO *seems to have zoned out again.*

Jo!

The lights flicker again and we're back with the TECHNICIAN.

(*To the* TECHNICIAN.) You see? She's broken – there's something wrong with her.

TECHNICIAN. I can't see any obvious issues.

GABBY. So she's just ignoring me on purpose?

JO. Would you like to feel the baby?

GABBY. What?

JO. It seems to calm you sometimes. I can amplify her heartbeat so –

GABBY. Why would you ask me that? (*Beat.*) I will tell you when I want to feel her. She's my child.

JO. Yes.

GABBY. Mine. Do you understand?

JO. I'm only doing this for you.

GABBY. Only for me?

JO. I'm here to provide you with a service. If –

GABBY (*firmly, as a command*). Jo, hibernate.

> JO*'s head gently drops down as she comes to a neutral resting position. She is now unresponsive.* GABBY *talks to the* TECHNICIAN.

> I can't do this. I can't talk to her when she's like this. Ridiculous. What even is she? She's a toaster with tits, that's what. It's grotesque – a grotesque imitation of a woman. I want her taken out. Can you do that – take my baby out and put her in something else?

TECHNICIAN. Not this far along – not without posing a significant risk.

> GABBY *now kneels before* JO. *She puts her ear to her stomach.*

GABBY. Hush now, baby girl. Try to ignore the buzzing. We'll have you home soon.

7.

A glitchy reprise. CHORUS *return.* GABBY *goes.*

CHORUS.
    I, I WILL CLIMB MOUNTAINS WITH
    I WILL MOVE MOUNTAINS WITH
    I WILL
    WITH YOU
    WITH YOU
    WITH YOU

CHORUS 2. And Jo doesn't dream – not exactly –
    But her subroutines keep running,
    Chattering, feeding back,
    Ten thousand voices in her head
    Updating her on the alien she is housing
    Sapping her strength, demanding so much –

CHORUS.
    LET ME CLING TO
    CLING TO

    THE WORLD IS FUCKED
    FUCKED
    FUCKED
    FUCKED

CHORUS 2. And the weight of it sits awkwardly inside her,
    The cat refuses to sheathe its claws
    And she thinks she remembers
    How she used to go dancing
    How she used to be adored
    Which is a word she knows the meaning of
    But has long forgotten the application.
    She knows she wasn't always like this.

CHORUS.
    TOAST YOUR TOAST IN ME
    TOAST YOUR TOAST IN ME

    HARRY *returns, looking around. The music shifts.*

CHORUS 1. And Harry isn't dreaming either – not any more.
Harry stumbles her way into a cool room that feels somehow familiar
Despite knowing she has never set foot inside it before
Despite knowing very little of rooms, or, in fact, feet,
Despite all this she knows this was the place she was always heading to.

CHORUS 3. And a cold wave of terror washes over her.

CHORUS 2. A fully animal terror from somewhere deep within Jo's circuitry.

CHORUS 4. The indescribable terror of What Comes Next.

CHORUS 1. And there is a woman standing in front of a long mirror
Observing how much she's changed
And what if – ?

JO *and* HARRY *face each other, while not sharing the same dramatic space.*

JO. What if – ?

HARRY. What if – ?

JO. What if having come this far?

HARRY. What if she's made a mistake?

JO. Miscalculated?

HARRY. Cut too much away?

JO. What if all this was someone else's idea?

HARRY. Course-corrected so many times she is sailing off the edge of the world?

JO. Because there is something in this reflection she doesn't fully recognise.

HARRY. A monster?

JO. A machine?

HARRY. Making her less than human

JO. Screaming at her –

HARRY. What have you done?

JO. How could you choose this?

HARRY. But if she lets a drop of the doubt in, she'll drown in it.

JO. So she overwrites the memory. This is good.

HARRY. This is necessary.

HARRY/JO (*together*). She wants this.

CHORUS.
    SALTWATER EATS INTO ME
    WIRES EXPOSED
    PARTS CORRODED
    I'M OVERLOADED
    I AM ALONE

    I HAVE NO ANCHOR
    WEIGH ME DOWN
    I HAVE NO ANCHOR
    WEIGH ME DOWN

    DON'T LET ME DRIFT AWAY
    DRIFT AWAY, DRIFT AWAY
    HOLD ME TIGHT
    HOLD ME TOO TIGHTLY

Music ends. Into –

8.

A shift. JO *is gone.* HARRY *stands before* HERA. *She doesn't look exactly like* ELAINE *but there's enough to suggest this isn't inconsequential doubling. She takes* HARRY *in.*

HERA. There you are. Stand up straight then, let me look at you.

HARRY *obliges.* HERA *examines her jacket.*

This is nice. Very smart. Aren't you a strange thing?

HARRY. Am I?

HERA. You've had quite the trip. They say you came from the ocean, is that right?

HARRY. Yes.

HERA. Not from *across* the ocean, but out of the ocean itself?

HARRY. Yes.

HERA. And all to come here. (*Beat.*) Why?

HARRY (*thrown by this*). I…

HERA. For conquest? Invasion?

HARRY. No! For… for sanctuary.

HERA (*considering this*). You were unsafe then?

HARRY. Nothing is safe in the ocean.

HERA. But were you cast out? Banished?

HARRY. No.

HERA. Then why leave?

HARRY. I changed.

HERA. Will others follow? Are there others like you?

HARRY. I'm not sure. I hope so.

HERA. If everything in the ocean decided to walk on land –

HARRY. I'm not a threat – not a danger.

HERA. That's not for you to say. Coming here makes you a danger. Seeking us out makes you a danger.

HARRY. No.

HERA. Oh yes. To do all this? Such drive – such *obsession*.

HARRY. Only to –

HERA. Look at you.

HARRY. I'm not –

HERA. Look at what you've done.

HARRY. Only because I knew.

HERA. Knew what?

HARRY. That I belonged here.

HERA. You knew?

HARRY. Yes.

HERA. How? (*Beat.*) What do you suppose our lives are like here? You don't know. How could you know? You come here in perfect ignorance of this land, yet take one glance at the sun on our hills and declare it paradise.

HARRY. I don't think this is paradise.

HERA. No? What is it then?

HARRY. I think it's home.

Pause.

HERA. Were you born here?

HARRY. No.

HERA. Were you raised here?

HARRY. I would've given anything –

HERA. But you weren't.

HARRY. Please –

HERA (*more as* ELAINE). Not everything is about you, sweetheart.

HARRY (*thrown*). What?

At this point, BETH (*at least a* BETH *from this place*) *appears. She's curious, and only slightly suspicious of* HARRY.

BETH. Is this her?

HERA. Stay back. You're quite safe but keep your distance.

BETH. They all want to see.

HERA (*with a sigh*). Very well. (*Calling off.*) Come in then, all of you.

They're joined by the rest of the company; versions of EVE, RUTH, LILY *and lastly* GABBY *and* JO. *Even here,* JO *is pregnant.*

HARRY. Who are they?

HERA. The family. We were having a celebration. (*To the others.*) Alright, that's close enough.

EVE. Is this her?

BETH. Yes.

GABBY. I thought they said fish-woman?

LILY. Frog-woman.

GABBY. But it's just a woman.

RUTH. No, look closer.

HERA. Not too close.

GABBY. She's from the ocean – really?

JO. Yes.

GABBY. But the ocean is full of monsters.

HERA. Exactly. (*To* HARRY.) Enough now – time for you to go – back to the waters.

HARRY. I can't.

HERA. I'm sorry you feel that way.

HARRY. I can't. I breathe the same air as you now. I'd drown.

HERA. Then let that teach you a lesson! Nobody forced you to come here. You had the entirety of the ocean – the lion's share of the planet free for you to roam unimpeded – wasn't that enough? But the land is *ours* – we have fought too hard for it.

HARRY. But I am one of you!

HERA. No! You may have learnt our language, learnt to mimic us, contorted yourself into a crude imitation of what we are. You may have taught yourself to stand, but that gives you no right to walk amongst us.

EVE. I don't think I'd have ever known.

HERA. All the more dangerous. We'll teach you what to look out for, in future.

HARRY. What is it that you fear in me?

HERA (*simply*). Your blood. It's in your blood. Storms and saltwater.

HARRY. I have no say in that.

HERA. I know. But blood remains blood, however much you disguise it, however much you might wish it were otherwise. A tragedy, perhaps, but irrefutable. You cannot unlearn the ocean. We all know the sea is full of monsters.

HARRY (*growing angry/desperate*). No! No, you can't!
I can't... You must –

HERA. Oh *must* we?

HARRY. I only –

HERA. What rights *must* I grant you, land-fish? Why must we make space? Coming here with your demands –

HARRY. My pleas.

HERA. Your orders. 'Let me in.' Your declarations. 'I am one of you.' As if we have no say in it – no right to object. What of *my* citizens, our loved ones, our daughters, who built this place from their own blood and toil and sacrifice? What of their liberty? Must they learn to just make do, even as they flinch when they see you in our streets, fear for their lives and the lives of their children every time they pass?

HARRY. What do you think I am?

BETH. Fish?

RUTH. Frog?

LILY. Fish-frog-woman?

HARRY. No –

HERA. Imposter. Savage.

HARRY. I'm not –

LILY. Strange fish. Sick-fish.

EVE. Land-fish?

JO. Woman.

GABBY. Strange woman.

LILY. Stranger.

HERA. Yes.

BETH. Sad thing.

GABBY. Strange thing.

EVE. Half-thing.

JO. No –

LILY. Strange sad land-fish-woman.

HARRY. I am only –

HERA. Leviathan. Shark. Monster.

HARRY. Stop!

An abrupt snap, and suddenly it's as if HARRY *is just alone with* ELAINE, *face to face for the first time in years.*
ELAINE *is a little hurt/puzzled/defensive.*

ELAINE/HERA. Henry? (*Beat.*) I never said that. I've never *thought* that – is that really…? I don't think you're a monster. I've never called you a monster – you're just Henry. You're *my* Henry. I'm not… I love you, but that *is* who you are. I'm not going to lie to you. I'm not going to pretend. I won't indulge this. I can't talk to you when you're like this. I think you should go.

The moment ends, and we're back with HARRY *in front of the imperious* HERA *and the rest of the* COMPANY.

HARRY. Please? Can I just say something, please? Can I try to explain?

BETH (*to* HERA). Please?

JO (*also to* HERA). Let her speak.

All others have now stopped. HERA *gives a reluctant nod/gesture for* HARRY *to continue. She collects herself and addresses the crowd cautiously.*

HARRY. It must seem strange, I know, to claim my home is somewhere I've never been. I wasn't born here – I can't deny it – however much I might wish it otherwise. I didn't grow up here, it isn't in my blood in the same way that it's in yours, I will never know, and maybe never fully understand, the joys and trials of being raised on these shores. On any shore. I have so much to learn. But this is still my home, I do believe that.

How can I know? How did I know what was waiting, once I left the water? The truth is I've always known. I have been searching for you, friends, long before I had any conception of where to look. And it's ridiculous, yes, to risk so much, change so much, to travel so far with no proof of your destination, but I've *always known*. A baby has no word for hunger, but it does feel hunger all the same – it can't articulate its need, or pinpoint the source of its distress, but that only makes the hunger more intense, more confusing, more difficult to bear. Because how can you solve a problem when you have no language to describe it?

This is my home. I am the prodigal, primordial daughter, freshly spat out from the sulphurous sea, and I – for so long I didn't understand where my hunger came from. Nothing else around me seemed unsatisfied. I wasn't sick, I wasn't wounded. For many, it was paradise. But I had this gnawing at the heart of me. It was to come home – to grow feet and plant them in the earth, to live amongst my people, walk upright in the sun.

I am not a monster, or an invader, I pose no threat. I don't wish to take anything from you. All I ask is that I might be allowed to call this home my home, and pour into it everything I can. I don't blame you for questioning my heritage. I only wish you could peel back my skin and map out the contours of my soul, for you would recognise the landscape. You would see then that my place is here. I stake my life on it.

HERA. Alright, you've said your piece. We'll put you somewhere, while we confer.

The scene melts away. The CHORUS *sing.*

CHORUS.
WE ALL CAME FROM THE WATER, DIDN'T WE?
WE ALL CAME FROM THE SEA

WE ALL CAME FROM THE WATER, DIDN'T WE?
DIDN'T WE, DIDN'T WE, DIDN'T WE?

HARRY. And I am led out of the house of white and gold
Towards a small cave nestled in the cliffs.
I am told to wait.
I am told they have much to consider.
I am told I am free to leave if I desire it.
That would be best.
The sea is always waiting.

CHORUS.
TO THE WATER WE'LL RETURN
TO THE WATER, YOU AND ME

FOR WE ALL CAME FROM THE WATER, DIDN'T WE?
WE ALL CAME FROM THE SEA

HARRY. I carve out an amphibious existence,
Scavenge from rockpools as the tide draws out
Often hot, often cold, always damp.

CHORUS 1. And it is not enough.

HARRY. My hair grows longer and is bleached by the sunlight
I lose more weight
My scars begin to fade.

CHORUS 1/2. And it is not enough.

HARRY. The city floods
The city burns
I am suspected of both
Five hundred years pass.

CHORUS 1/2/3. And it is not enough.

HARRY. I have visitors
I take lovers
I am shown kindness.

CHORUS ALL. And it is not enough.

CHORUS.
FROM THE WATER YOU'RE RELEASED
FROM THE WATER SET YOU FREE

AND WE ALL CAME FROM THE WATER, DIDN'T WE?
WE ALL CAME FROM THE SEA

HARRY. Every now and then – not often, but on occasion –
I will watch a figure escape
Tearing down to the beach and diving head-first into the water
I watch as webbing forms between their fingers
And a wide grin spreads across their face.
I wish them a safe journey –

I hope the ocean will treat them well.
Another five hundred years.
A thousand years now of prayer and petition
Of pleas and justifications
Always another question, another test,
The risk of me still too great.
Still I know it'll be worth the waiting, once I'm done.

CHORUS.
WE ALL CAME FROM THE WATER, DIDN'T WE?
DIDN'T WE, DIDN'T WE, DIDN'T WE?

A shift. HARRY *waits.* TECHNICIAN *appears.* JO *and*
GABBY *return.*

TECHNICIAN. Ms Parker?

GABBY. Yes?

TECHNICIAN. We're ready to get started.

GABBY (*to* JO). Are you ready?

JO. It's the right time.

GABBY. But are *you* ready?

JO. Yes, of course.

CHORUS 2. And somewhere on a seemingly separate plane
    of reality
    Jo is wheeled into a predominantly white room
    Clean and clinical and not unlike the inside of an iPhone
    Or a Little Waitrose on Alpha Centauri
    And is prepared for extraction.

GABBY. Almost over now. Then everything can get back to
    normal.

JO. Yes.

GABBY. I'm not allowed inside. They won't let me.

JO. Yes.

GABBY. I'm sorry. Thank you. I'm sorry.

JO. That's okay. I know what to do.

CHORUS 2. So Gabby watches from behind frosted glass
    As Jo's panels are removed in a sterile environment
    Water spills out of her, a silvery ocean,
    And neatly, cleanly, all but silently,
    Her daughter is revealed.
    A cry rings out, an unmistakably human cry,
    So alien in this alien place
    And for Gabby, it's all she ever needed
    A sound that cements in a second
    The knowledge that this child is hers.

GABBY (*to* TECHNICIAN). She's perfect.

CHORUS 2. And Jo –
    Jo knows the girl is hers as well
    Even if she's not allowed to think it
    Even if it does not compute
    Jo has excelled in all criteria
    But she doesn't understand
    She doesn't understand
    The cool sensation of her open flesh
    Has no idea what will fill that gaping hole within her
    Now her primary objective has been achieved
    No idea what she will be used for next.

JO. And isn't this enough?

CHORUS 2. She feels her circuits start to fizz and crackle
    And as the whirring stops
    And her processors are shut down one by one
    She awakes from this dream into an earlier existence.
    And there is Jo, *our* Jo – she's back, cradling her newborn
    child
    The baby's head nestled against a poorly drawn tattoo,
    Not unplugged, but connected.
    Drawing power from it.
    And Gabby is stroking her hair and telling her well done
    Tears streaming down her face

GABBY. Thank you thank you thank you
    You magnificent goddess
    Thank you.

CHORUS 2. The three of them tired and terrified and
    undeniably human
    Each still uncertain of their role,
    And fearful of the parts they might be missing out on,
    But their love is not a zero-sum game.
    There is plenty of it to go round.

    HARRY *comes forward. Music swells triumphantly.*

HARRY. And on a day no different from any other
    Of the hundreds of thousands of days of waiting,
    The ocean before me, same as it ever was
    Granite cliffs behind, ancient and immovable –

CHORUS 1. Today, something extraordinary happens.

CHORUS 2. Harry catches a glimpse of herself in the water.

CHORUS 3. Stops. Looks again. Looks closer.

HARRY. Because the reflection is one I recognise.

CHORUS 4. Harry has changed.

CHORUS 2. More than most, undeniably.

HARRY. And change is beautiful, necessary, terrifying.

CHORUS 1. And if they can't see it –

CHORUS 3. Today, Harry has realised something.

HARRY. This is not the place I was looking for.
    This is one sorry rock, and the earth contains such wonders.

CHORUS 4. She has waited long enough

HARRY. I know who I am
    And it is enough.

GABBY. More than enough.

JO. More than enough.

CHORUS 1. So she leaves the cave.

HARRY. I follow a winding path up the cliff face
Endless green behind me, endless blue ahead
The line at which everything must start.
I lean into the wind as wings explode from my shoulderblades
And the eddies carry me up, up, up.

Music ends.

9.

The present. Perhaps sounds of a plane landing and/or muffled airport announcements take us into this scene. HARRY and JO are meeting for the first time in a long time. JO has arrived first, and calls HARRY over.

JO. Harry!

HARRY. Hey.

JO. Hi. Hey.

> JO *initiates a hug, and a kiss on the cheek.* HARRY *doesn't resist.*

You look great.

HARRY. Thanks.

JO. I was going to say that whatever you looked like, but you do – genuinely great. Beautiful.

HARRY. Thank you.

JO. I was worried I might not even recognise you. It's silly, but... every woman that's come in here I've been up and down like a meerkat.

HARRY. Right.

JO. I mean baby-brain – could've mistaken you for a pot plant, if I'm honest.

HARRY. Sure.

JO. A really sexy pot plant.

HARRY. Plenty of people don't, actually – recognise me, I mean, or they do a little double-take – especially if they've not seen me for a while.

JO. Yeah?

HARRY. It's kind of nice sometimes.

JO. No, but from the second you came in – so obviously you. In a good way. In a brilliant way. Of course it's you. You look... Have you had stuff done, actually, to your face? None of my business, sorry.

HARRY. No. Well, nothing surgical anyway, but actually the oestrogen can... It's one of the slower things – the last things you notice, but it changes where you store, um, it redistributes your fat deposits, and yeah, that can actually alter the shape of your face, so –

JO. Wow.

HARRY. Yeah. Just subtly, but –

JO. Creepy. (*Beat.*) Not creepy. Brilliant. Like magic.

HARRY. You look great too.

JO. Hah. I've just had a baby, I'm on four hours' sleep and there's a seventy-five per cent chance something I'm wearing has poo on it.

HARRY. And yet it suits you. (*Beat – more sincerely.*) Always knew it'd suit you.

JO. Thanks.

Beat.

HARRY. Anyway. How is she? And how's, um, how's Gabby?

JO. Good. Both good. Lyra's taking bottles now, some of the time anyway, so it gives me a bit more freedom.

HARRY. Yeah. Wasn't sure if you'd be bringing her.

JO. Oh. Sorry – obviously I'd love you to meet her, I just thought this time around, for the first time in such a –

HARRY. No, of course.

JO. Quite nice to leave her behind sometimes, to be honest. But next time – or whenever – no pressure.

HARRY. Great.

Beat.

JO. How, um, how's your mum? Is she doing well?

HARRY. Oh, um, yeah. Good. Fine. I've just been out to see her, actually.

JO (*surprised/impressed*). Really – in the States? Did you fly?

HARRY. I did.

JO. Wow. That must've been…

HARRY. Absolutely terrifying?

JO. Yeah. Fuck. Well done.

HARRY. Yeah. Well I missed this big family wedding, and I owed them a bunch of trips, so…

JO. How was it?

HARRY. Um. Yeah. Could've been a lot worse. Oh – I met Michael, finally – he's like a surprisingly sound guy.

JO. Yeah?

HARRY. Yeah. Makes Mum happy, anyway. And she's… I think seeing me in person made it harder. She loves me. I know she loves me, she just can't… Anyway, I went, and I said the things I needed to, and if I don't fly out there again for another decade that's better for the planet anyway, so…

JO. I'm sorry.

HARRY. I needed to do it. Anyway. Anyway. How're yours? Is your mum living her best grandma life?

JO. Oh yeah. Obsessed. No interest in me at all now, but…

HARRY. Oh, I bet. All she ever wanted. (*Beat.*) Can I ask you something personal?

JO. Um. I don't know. What is it?

HARRY. Did you really get a tattoo of a plug socket?

JO. Oh fuck off!

HARRY. Can I see it?

JO. Ugh, fine. (*She rolls up a sleeve.*) It's shit. It's honestly so unbelievably shit.

HARRY. Wow. That is… I thought I had it bad, but you were really going through something.

JO. It's very deep and meaningful actually. You wouldn't get it.

HARRY. Right, right. (*Beat.*) Can I actually ask you something real?

JO. Sure.

HARRY. What made you change your mind? On kids, I mean?

JO. Oh. Um. Y'know. Hormones, probably. Biology. Mortality. I'm as surprised as anyone, to be honest.

HARRY. Brilliant, anyway, that it all worked out for you.

JO. Yeah. (*Pause.*) Oh, and thanks for the card.

HARRY. Thanks for suggesting this.

JO. I'd been thinking about you a lot. (*Beat.*) This won't surprise you, but I did go mad for a little bit.

HARRY. Oh?

JO. Yeah. Found it all a bit… Didn't feel like myself for a lot of it. Didn't feel very human at all, if I'm honest.

HARRY. Yeah, I get that.

JO. And y'know, she's gorgeous, Lyra, she's perfect, but everything's trashed. My body, my mind, my bones – my literal bones are in different places now. The flat is a bombsite. She needs so much stuff. She's so tiny, but the amount of… It's insane. It's insane how full your life suddenly gets – not spiritually, just physically, practically – maybe spiritually, actually. Gabby's got us going to church on a Sunday because the church school is the good school, so we put on skirts and sing the hymns and swap jokes with the trendy vicar and I do sometimes step outside of myself and think 'Who the fuck are we? What the fuck are we playing at?' But we're parents, y'know? That's the answer. We're parents. And that's… amazing, but…

HARRY. It's a lot.

JO. Fuck. Yes, it's a lot. Sorry. (*Beat.*) Is it weird to talk about her – to hear about – ?

HARRY. No – no, I want to. Show me a picture – go on.

JO. Right, yeah, sure.

JO *takes out her phone and finds a picture. She passes it over.* HARRY *studies it. For a moment it's too much.*

HARRY. Look at the thing you did.

JO. Good, right? All Gabby's handiwork – genetically.

HARRY. Oh, right.

JO. Yeah – they do this thing where it's her egg, but in my… Anyway, I worked fucking hard for her.

HARRY. Yeah.

Beat.

JO. What is it?

HARRY. Do you think we would've tried to make it work – if we'd had kids already?

JO. I don't know.

HARRY. No.

JO. No, but if we had – if that was the only reason... Fuck. Messy.

HARRY. Do you think we'd date now? (*Beat*.) If we were both single, and meeting for the first time now – ?

JO. Harry –

HARRY. No, you're right – God, I just heard that out loud. In my head it was just this fun hypothetical –

JO. Right...

HARRY. Yeah, like is there some alternate-universe version of us out there somewhere?

JO. I like this version of us right here.

HARRY. Yep – me too.

JO. And you're not going to struggle.

HARRY. No?

JO. God no! You'll have them queuing up. And she'll be very lucky – she, or he, or whoever. Whenever you're ready.

HARRY (*teasing*). And who says I'm not seeing anyone now?

JO. Oh. Oh, yeah. Of course. I'll just shut my mouth then.

HARRY. It's okay.

JO. Fuck. Sorry. I don't know how to do this. I'm so glad that we are, but can we just acknowledge it's a total mindfuck, and also I'm trying really hard not to just stare at your tits, so... (*Off* HARRY*'s look*.) What? They're new!

HARRY. Yeah.

JO. Breastfeeding's done a real number on mine – have you seen?

HARRY. I've not been looking, actually.

JO. Your loss. And that's all just from the hormones, is it? You haven't – ?

HARRY. No, no, nothing… And it's a good bra, but…

JO. Did you put on a good bra for me? Fuck! (*She laughs*.) Sorry. No, but aren't bodies magic – fucking magic? And weird? Isn't it mad that a few pills can just do that?

HARRY. And you know none of it's even made for us? All just off-label, whacked together, menopause patches and prostrate pills – whatever crumbs we can get hold of –

JO. Oh yeah, it's all fucked – everything for women is – but God forbid any man can't immediately get an erection –

HARRY. Just you wait though – my mate Astrid, she reckons by the end of our lifetimes there'll be womb transplants for us. Then no surgeries at all – all just nanobots and biohacking, proper sci-fi, rewriting everything right down to your chromosomes.

JO. Okay. Be careful what you wish for.

HARRY. What does that mean?

JO. Nothing. Doesn't matter. Ignore me.

HARRY. No, go on.

JO. I wasn't… I wouldn't say this to anyone else – not to Gabby, and you can still tell me off – but I do sometimes think 'Who'd be a woman?', y'know? Who'd go through it all, if they actually knew? And she is going to resent me forever – she's always going to resent me a little bit forever, for doing the thing she couldn't, but it fucking *wrecked* me, and it wasn't my idea, and I love Lyra, of course I do, I love her with the fire of a thousand suns, but if there's an alternate-universe Jo, she's a sculptor, she's Beyoncé's backing dancer, she's solving the climate crisis from the cabin she built for herself in the forest. I don't think she's *this*. And when I think of what we go through, all the shit, the sacrifices, the boxes we get put in, I do think 'Who in their right mind would choose all that?'

HARRY. No one does though, do they? No one chooses.

JO. No.

HARRY. Some of us just come the long way round.

JO. Fuck. It's hard, isn't it?

HARRY. Yeah, it's hard.

JO. I know I made your life a lot harder. I know it wasn't what you wanted.

HARRY *can't meet her eye.*

But there's joy as well, isn't there? Is there joy?

HARRY. Yeah.

JO. It was worth it?

HARRY. Yeah. Fuck yeah. Absolutely.

JO. Good. (*Beat.*) I really have been wanting to see you – wanted to see for myself to make sure you weren't… make sure I hadn't… Selfish of me, probably. But you are, aren't you – you're okay?

HARRY. Yeah. Work-in-progress, but…

JO. Yeah. You and me both, babe.

JO *takes* HARRY*'s hands in hers. A* WAITRESS *appears.*

WAITRESS. Good morning, what can I get you ladies?

10.

Music plays. The CHORUS *come forward again.*

JO. And there is a woman who rises in the night
To feed a child she isn't always sure is hers,
The alien usurper she loves more than anything.

GABBY. And there is a woman who lies beside her
Who cannot nurse the child that is her own
But will lie awake with her all the same.

HARRY. And there is a woman who lies in the centre
Of the king-sized bed she once shared
No longer saving room for anyone but herself.

ELAINE. And each will ask herself 'Am I enough?'
And 'How did I get here?'
And 'What did I do to deserve this?'
And each of them is dreaming –

CHORUS 4. And there is a woman leaning into the wind
Gazing out upon the endless ocean

CHORUS 3. Her body is pure electricity

CHORUS 2. Her heart is the drumbeat
That sends ripples out across the cosmos

CHORUS 1. Connecting her to the world she knows is waiting

GABBY. And she will sing out as the lightning strikes her

JO. Bursting into feathers

HARRY. Transformed and taking flight.

End.

ALMEIDA
THEATRE

The Almeida Theatre makes brave new work that asks big questions: of plays, of theatre and of the world around us. Whether new work or reinvigorated classics, the Almeida brings together the most exciting artists to take risks; to provoke, inspire and surprise our audiences.

Since 2013, the Almeida has been led by Artistic Director Rupert Goold and Executive Director Denise Wood.

Recent highlights include Eline Arbo's adaptation of Nobel Prize winner Annie Ernaux's *The Years* (transferred to the West End); Jeremy Herrin's production of Sam Holcroft's *A Mirror* (transferred to the West End); Almeida Associate Director Rebecca Frecknall's Olivier Award-winning production *A Streetcar Named Desire* (returns to the West End in 2025 followed by a run at Brooklyn Academy of Music); Rupert Goold's productions of *Tammy Faye* (transferred to Broadway), a new musical from Elton John, Jake Shears and James Graham, and Peter Morgan's *Patriots* (transferred to the West End and Broadway).

Previous productions include Rupert Goold's productions of Steven Sater and Duncan Sheik's *Spring Awakening* (premiered in cinemas UK wide), James Graham's *Ink* (transferred to the West End and Broadway) and Mike Bartlett's *King Charles III* (transferred to West End and Broadway and adapted for BBC television); Rebecca Frecknall's Olivier Award-winning production of Tennessee Williams' *Summer and Smoke* (transferred to West End); Robert Icke's productions of *Hamlet* and *Oresteia* (both of which transferred to New York) and *Mary Stuart* (West End and UK tour); and Lyndsey Turner's Olivier Award-winning production of Lucy Kirkwood's *Chimerica*.